# Remember This?

*8/30/2022*

*Annalou*
*Grou:*
*Lunch Dr*

*People, Things and Events*
## FROM **1937** TO THE **PRESENT DAY**

US EDITION

With thanks for additional research by Larry Farr, Dana Lemay, Rose Myers and Idan Solon.

Baby statistics: Office of Retirement and Disability Policy, Social Security Administration.

Cover: Library of Congress: World Telegram photo by Roger Higgins LC-USZ62-117772, Anthony Angel Collection LC-DIG-ppmsca-69422; Mary Evans: Everett Collection, Keystone Pictures USA/zumapress.com. Icons from rawpixel/Freepik.

Cover Design: Fanni Williams / thehappycolourstudio.com

The Milestone Memories series including this *Remember This?* title is produced by Milestones Memories Press, a division of Say So Media Ltd.

First edition: October 2021
Updated: February 2022

We've tried our best to check our facts, but mistakes can still slip through. Spotted one? We'd love to know about it: info@saysomedia.net

# Rewind, Replay, Remember

What can you remember before you turned six? If you're like most of us, not much: the comforting smell of a blanket or the rough texture of a sweater, perhaps. A mental snapshot of a parent arriving home late at night. A tingle of delight or the shadow of sorrow.

But as we grow out of childhood, our autobiographical and episodic memories—they're the ones hitched to significant events such as birthdays or leaving school—are created and filed more effectively, enabling us to piece them together at a later date. And the more we revisit those memories, the less likely we are to lose the key that unlocks them.

We assemble these fragments into a more-or-less coherent account of our lives—the one we tell to ourselves, our friends, our relatives. And while this one-of-a-kind biopic loses a little definition over the years, some episodes remain in glorious technicolor—although it's usually the most embarrassing incidents!

But this is one movie that's never quite complete. Have you ever had a memory spring back unbidden, triggered by something seemingly unrelated? This book is an attempt to discover those forgotten scenes using the events, sounds, and faces linked to the milestones in your life.

It's time to blow off the cobwebs and see how much you can remember!

# It Happened in 1937

The biggest event in the year is one that didn't make the front pages: you were born! Here are some of the national stories that people were talking about.

- ✦ Krispy Kreme doughnuts go on sale
- ✦ Joe Louis becomes World Heavyweight Champion
- ✦ Golden Gate Bridge opens
- ✦ Ohio River floods
- ✦ New London School disaster kills 295 students and teachers
- ✦ Hindenburg airship explodes
- ✦ Amelia Earhart disappears (right)
- ✦ Oil magnate John D. Rockefeller died
- ✦ New York Yankees win the World Series
- ✦ Benny Goodman tops the radio playlists
- ✦ SPAM hits the grocery store shelves
- ✦ "World Spinach Capital"—Crystal City, TX—erects statue of Popeye
- ✦ Actor Ronald Reagan makes his film debut
- ✦ Cyclamate sweeteners developed
- ✦ National Basketball League founded
- ✦ Daffy Duck debuts
- ✦ First blood banks open
- ✦ Composer George Gershwin died
- ✦ Look magazine hits the newsstands

*Born this year:*
- ⚭ Actor Morgan Freeman
- ⚭ Comedian George Carlin
- ⚭ Actress Jane Fonda
- ⚭ Actor Jack Nicholson

In 1932—just four years after being the first woman to fly as a passenger across the Atlantic—Amelia Earhart made the journey on her own. "Have you flown far?" asked a farm worker who watched her land in Northern Ireland. "From America," Earhart replied.

Earhart had her own clothing line and celebrity endorsements; she became a friend of Eleanor Roosevelt, espoused equal rights, and held positions in academia. Her next goal was an equatorial circumnavigation. In 1937 she took the controls of her Lockheed 10-E Electra (above), alongside navigator Fred Noonan. On the final leg over the Pacific, they disappeared without a trace.

# On the Bookshelf When You Were Small

The books of our childhood linger long in the memory. These are the children's classics, all published in your first ten years. Do you remember the stories? What about the covers?

| | |
|---|---|
| 1937 | Adventures of the Wishing Chair by Enid Blyton |
| 1937 | And to Think That I Saw It on Mulberry Street by Dr. Seuss |
| 1937 | The Hobbit by J.R.R. Tolkien |
| 1938 | **Heidi Grows Up by Charles Tritten**<br>In 1881, Joahanna Spyri published one of the best-selling books of all time: Heidi. Fifty-five years later, Tritten–who had translated Heidi into French–wrote a sequel. It was published the year before Shirley Temple took to the screen as the braided Swiss orphan. |
| 1938 | The Sword in the Stone by T.H. White |
| 1938 | Mr. Popper's Penguins by Richard & Florence Atwater |
| 1939 | Anne of Ingleside by Lucy Maud Montgomery |
| 1940 | Lassie Come Home by Eric Knight |
| 1940 | Pat the Bunny by Dorothy Kunhardt |
| 1941 | The Black Stallion by Walter Farley |
| 1941 | Curious George by H.A. Rey |
| 1942 | Marshmallow by Clare Turlay Newberry |
| 1942 | The Runaway Bunny by Margaret Wise Brown |
| 1942 | The Poky Little Puppy by Janette Sebring Lowrey |
| 1943 | **The Little Prince by Antoine de Saint-Exupéry**<br>In 1935, poet, aristocrat and aviator de Saint-Exupéry crash-landed in the desert. His hallucinations before eventual rescue were the seeds of the story that would later become the bestseller Le Petit Prince. |
| 1944 | Mother Goose by Tasha Tudor |
| 1945 | Pippi Longstocking by Astrid Lindgren |
| 1945 | Stuart Little by E.B. White |
| 1946 | **Thomas the Tank Engine by Rev. W. Awdry**<br>Rev. Awdrey appeared in his own books as the Thin Clergyman. His more portly friend in real life, Teddy Boston, appeared by his fictional side–known, of course, as the Fat Clergyman. |

# Around the World in Your Birth Year

Here are the events from outside the US that were big enough to make news back home in the year you were born. And you won't remember any of them!

+ Carmina Burana premieres
+ Japan takes Shanghai
+ Ground tests performed on jet engine in England
+ Flying car takes first flight
+ Nanking massacre begins
+ Italian troops murder over 300 in Ethiopian monastery
+ Japan invades China
+ Typhoon hits Hong Kong
+ Brazilian president names himself dictator
+ Mitsubishi-built airplane flies from Japan to London
+ Workers go on strike all over Paris
+ King George VI becomes king of England
+ Volkswagen begins production
+ Neville Chamberlain becomes prime minister
+ Irish Free State's new constitution receives more votes
+ Bombs fall on Madrid
+ Italy withdraws from the League of Nations
+ Mine collapse kills over 245 people
+ Picasso paints Guernica
+ Duke of Windsor marries commoner
+ Pope Pius XI writes encyclical critical of communism
+ Soviet Union increases sending people to the Gulags
+ French government collapses
+ Longest eclipse (7 minutes), in 800 years, seen in Peru and the Pacific

# Boys' Names When You Were Born

Once upon a time, popular names came… and stuck. (John hogged the top spot for 40 years, to 1924.) These are the most popular names when you were born.

Robert
**James**
Robert topped the list in 1937 but the most popular boys' name of the last hundred years was James, bestowed upon nearly five million babies (narrowly beating John into second place overall).

John
William
Richard
Charles
Donald
George
Thomas
Joseph
David
Ronald
Edward
Paul
Kenneth
Frank
Raymond
Jack
Billy
Harold
Gerald
Jerry
Walter
Bobby

**Rising and falling stars:**
Jerome made his first Top 100 appearance in 1935, but he'd sunk without trace by 1940. Charlie slipped away in 1935, too.

# Girls' Names When You Were Born

On the girls' side of the ward, two names had reigned supreme for many years. By 1937, Helen had been usurped by Mary—but even her crown was wobbling...

### Mary
Mary took the top spot for girls over the last 100 years, but the distribution of girls' names is very different: "only" 3 million babies were named Mary, while second place Patricia was given to just 1.5 million infants (vs. 4.5 million for John).

### Shirley
1935-6 marked the high spot for Shirley: she's been slipping in the rankings ever since, falling out of the Top 100 in 1963.

Barbara
Betty
Patricia
Dorothy
Joan
Margaret
Nancy
Helen
Carol
Joyce
Doris
Marilyn
Ruth
Virginia
Elizabeth
Jean
Frances
Beverly
Lois
Janet

### Rising and falling stars:
Roberta, Sharon and Yvonne made their first Top 100 appearance in 1935 while Esther, Willie and Margie would never be seen again.

# Things People Did When You Were Growing Up...

...that hardly anyone does now. Some of these we remember fondly; others are best left in the past!

- ✦ Help Mom make cookies using a cookie press
- ✦ Keep bread in a breadbox
- ✦ Can and preserve vegetables from your garden
- ✦ Listen to daytime soap operas on the radio
- ✦ Participate in Church fundraisers
- ✦ Watch endurance competitions like flagpole sitting and goldfish eating
- ✦ Build scooters from roller skates and scrap wood
- ✦ Bring a slide-rule to math class
- ✦ Take a Sunday drive out to the country
- ✦ Play leapfrog
- ✦ Live in a Sears Modern Home ordered from the Sears catalog
- ✦ Get a treat from the pharmacy soda fountain
- ✦ Camp in a "Hooverville" while looking for work
- ✦ Keep a thrift or kitchen garden
- ✦ Buy penny candy
- ✦ Buy goods from door-to-door salesmen
- ✦ Wear clothing made from flour sacks
- ✦ Collect marbles
- ✦ Join a dance marathon
- ✦ Listen to Amos n' Andy on the radio on weekend evenings
- ✦ Eat Water Pie
- ✦ "Window shop" downtown on Saturdays
- ✦ Pitch pennies
- ✦ Earn $30 a month plus food and shelter working for the Civilian Conservation Corps

# How Many of These Games Are Still Played?

The first half of the 20th century was the heyday for new board and card games launched to the US public. Some are still firm family favorites, but which ones did you play when you were young?

| | |
|---|---|
| 1925 | Pegity |
| 1925 | Playing for the Cup |
| 1927 | Hokum ("The game for a roomful") |
| 1920s | The Greyhound Racing Game |
| 1930 | Wahoo |
| 1932 | Finance |
| 1934 | Sorry! |
| 1935 | **Monopoly**<br>The game's origins lie with The Landlord's Game, patented in 1904 by Elizabeth Magie. (The anti-monopoly version–Prosperity–didn't catch on.) It was the first game with a never-ending path rather than a fixed start and finish. |
| 1935 | Easy Money |
| 1936 | The Amazing Adventures of Fibber McGee |
| 1937 | Meet the Missus |
| 1937 | Stock Ticker |
| 1938 | Scrabble |
| 1938 | Movie Millions |
| 1940 | Dig |
| 1940 | Prowl Car |
| 1942 | Sea Raider |
| 1943 | Chutes and Ladders |
| 1949 | **Clue**<br>Clue–or Cluedo, as it is known to most outside the USA–introduced us to a host of shady characters and grisly murder weapons. For years those included a piece of genuine lead pipe, now replaced on health grounds. |
| 1949 | **Candy Land**<br>This wholesome family racing game, invented on a polio ward, was the victim of something less savory nearly 50 years after its launch when an adult website claimed the domain name. Thankfully, the courts swiftly intervened. |

# Things People Do Now...

...that were virtually unknown when you were young.
How many of these habits are part of your routine or even
second nature these days? Do you remember the first time?

- Get curbside grocery pickup
- Stream movies instead of going to Blockbuster for a rental
- Learn remotely and online
- Communicate by text or video chat
- Use a Kindle or other e-reading device
- Go geocaching
- Track your sleep, exercise, or fertility with a watch
- Use a weighted blanket
- Use a robotic/automatic vacuum
- Take your dog to a dog park
- Have a package delivered by drone
- Find a date online or through an app
- Use hand sanitizer
- Automatically soothe your baby with a self-rocking bassinet
- Host a gender-reveal party during pregnancy
- Use a home essential oil diffuser or salt lamp
- Have a "destination wedding"
- Use a device charging station while waiting for a flight
- Get a ride from Uber or Lyft instead of a taxi
- Drink hard seltzer
- Take a home DNA test (for you... or your pet)
- Have a telemedicine/virtual healthcare visit
- Smoke an e-cigarette/"vape"
- Start your car, dryer, or air conditioner via an app

# Popular Food in the 1950s

For many, the post-war years meant more of one thing in particular on the table: meat. In the yard, men stepped up to the barbeque to sharpen their skills. In the kitchen, fancy new electric appliances and frozen TV dinners promised convenience and new, exotic flavors.

Tuna noodle casserole
Dinty Moore Beef Stew
Beef stroganoff
**Green bean casserole**
Green bean casserole was invented in the Campbell's test kitchen in 1955 as a cheap, fuss-free dish. Today, around 40 percent of Campbell's Cream of Mushroom soup sold in the US goes into this dinner table staple.

**Pigs-in-a-blanket**
Pigs get different blankets in the United Kingdom, where sausages are wrapped in bacon rather than pastry.

Backyard barbecues
Ovaltine
Swedish meatballs
Pineapple upside down cake
**Spam**
Ground pork shoulder and ham sold in a distinctive can—for much of the world, that means Spam. This "meatloaf without basic training" is affordable and still popular, with over eight billion cans sold since it was first sold in 1937.

Ambrosia salad
Sugar Smacks
Cheez Whiz
Stuffed celery
Campbell's Tomato Soup spice cake
**Swanson Turkey TV Dinners**
Dreamed up as a solution to an over-supply of turkey, TV dinners proved nearly as popular as the TV itself. Swanson sold over 25 million of them in 1954, the year these handy meal packs were launched.

Veg-All canned vegetables
Chicken à la King

# Cars of the 1950s

Was this the golden age of automobiles? In truth, some of these models had been brought to market long before, such as the Buick Roadmaster and the Studebaker Champion. But even stalwarts were quick to adopt the Space Age theme of the decade as sweeping lines, tailfins, and cascading chrome grilles became the norm.

| | |
|---|---|
| 1926 | Chrysler Imperial |
| 1936 | General Motors Buick Roadmaster |
| 1939 | **Studebaker Champion**<br>Over seven decades, the Champion's creator, Raymond Loewy, designed railroads, logos, buses, vending machines, and a space station for NASA. |
| 1939 | Chrysler DeSoto Custom |
| 1947 | Studebaker Starlight Coupe |
| 1948 | **Crosley Station Wagon**<br>The first car to be marketed as "Sports Utility." |
| 1948 | Jaguar XK120 |
| 1949 | **Muntz Jet**<br>Fewer than 200 Muntz Jets were built by founder Madman Muntz, an engineer who married seven times and made (and lost) fortunes selling cars, TVs, and more. |
| 1949 | Chrysler Dodge Coronet |
| 1950 | General Motors Chevrolet Bel-Air |
| 1950 | Nash Rambler |
| 1951 | Hudson Hornet |
| 1953 | General Motors Chevrolet Corvette |
| 1953 | General Motors Buick Skylark |
| 1953 | General Motors Cadillac Eldorado |
| 1953 | Nash Metropolitan |
| 1954 | Ford Skyliner |
| 1955 | Ford Thunderbird |
| 1955 | Ford Fairlane |
| 1956 | Studebaker Golden Hawk |
| 1956 | Chrysler Plymouth Fury |
| 1957 | **Mercedes-Benz 300 SL Roadster**<br>Voted "Sports Car of the Century" in 1999. |

Cars crawl out of 1950s Philadelphia over the Ben Franklin Bridge. Henry Ford wasn't the only one to "build a car for the great multitude." Millions of new suburbanites embraced their newfound freedom—even if that meant driving to the same place as everyone else.

# Fashion in the Fifties

How much do you remember of Fifties fashion? Reminders of this fast-changing time are everywhere as today's fashions consciously reference the icons, designers and subcultures of the era. Here they all are, from rockabilly to pin-ups and poodle to pencil.

### Bullet or torpedo bra
Bullet bras were the bras of choice for "Sweater Girls" such as Patti Page, Marilyn Monroe and Lana Turner.

### Bomber jackets
The iconic bomber jacket is the US Army Air Corps A2. These A2 jackets were made to be so durable that originals still exist today, some in good condition.

Penny loafer shoes

Pencil skirt

### Cristóbal Balenciaga
Publicity-shy Balenciaga gave just one interview in his life, preferring to let his well-fitting clothes do the talking. His models were known as the 'monsters'—a poor moniker for women of different shapes, ages and demeanours.

Hawaiian "Aloha" shirt

Tea length swing dresses

Corduroy pants/slacks

### Poodle skirt
Actress and singer Juli Lynne Charlot created the poodle skirt in a last-minute effort to put together an outfit for a Christmas party. Her design didn't require sewing; just a circle of felt and some fun appliqués! Charlot soon had many requests for her poodle skirts, and her fashion company was born soon after.

Kitten heel shoes

Peter Pan collar blouses

Capri pants

Coco Chanel

Hubert de Givenchy

Silk or chiffon scarf

Clubmaster sunglasses

Christian Dior

# Faster, Easier, Better

Yesterday's technological breakthrough is today's modern convenience. Here are some of the lab and engineering marvels that were made before you turned 21 years old.

| | |
|---|---|
| 1937 | Polarized sunglasses |
| 1938 | Teflon |
| 1938 | Samsung founded—as a grocery store |
| 1939 | Regular TV broadcasts begin |
| 1940 | Color Television |
| 1941 | Electric guitar (solid body) |
| 1942 | **Toilet paper** |

Until 1942, the best you could hope for from your toilet paper was that it was splinter-free. But in a big boost to their bottom line, a paper mill in England began to offer two-ply toilet paper for a softer touch.

| | |
|---|---|
| 1943 | Kidney dialysis machine |
| 1944 | Programmable calculator |
| 1945 | Cruise control in cars |
| 1946 | **Waterproof diaper** |

The inventor of the first waterproof diaper, the Boater, was told repeatedly that no one wanted it and no one had been asking for such a thing. She decided to manufacture it herself and the product was an immediate success.

| | |
|---|---|
| 1947 | Transistor |
| 1948 | Computer program |
| 1949 | Wurlitzer Select-O-Matic jukebox |
| 1949 | Zamboni ice resurfacer |
| 1950 | Teleprompter |
| 1951 | Wetsuit |
| 1952 | Artificial heart |
| 1953 | Heart-lung machine |
| 1954 | Acoustic suspension loudspeaker |
| 1955 | Pocket transistor radio |
| 1956 | Hard Disk Drive |
| 1956 | Operating system (OS) |
| 1957 | Laser |

# Across the Nation

**10**

Double digits at last: you're old enough to eavesdrop on adults and scan the headlines. These may be some of the earliest national news stories you remember.

+ "Black Dahlia" murdered
+ African American newsman covers Congress
+ Animals launched into space
+ Polaroid demonstrates instant camera
+ Langer's Deli opens
+ Best Year of Our Lives wins Best Picture
+ Jackie Robinson takes the field
+ Tony Awards begin
+ Texas City explosion
+ Term "Cold War" coined
+ Truman Doctrine signed
+ Marshall Plan outlined
+ UFOs sighted, "Men in Black" reportedly issue warning to remain quiet
+ Roswell crash
+ House Un-American Activities Committee begins investigating
+ Television broadcast the New York Yankees World Series win
+ Chuck Yeager breaks the sound barrier
+ Meet the Press airs
+ Missouri town receives a foot of rainfall in under 45 minutes
+ Transistor invented
+ Spruce Goose flies
+ Everglades National Park dedicated

*Born this year:*
&ᴘ Author Stephen King
&ᴘ First Lady Hillary Clinton

# Kapow! Comic Books and Heroes from Your Childhood

Barely a year went past in the mid-20th Century without a new super-powered hero arriving to save the day. Here are some that were taking on the bad guys during your childhood.

Police Comics ✷ Plastic Man
More Fun Comics ✷ Green Arrow
Super Rabbit Comics ✷ Super Rabbit
Terrytoons Comics ✷ Mighty Mouse
Millie The Model ✷ Millie
All Star Comics ✷ Justice Society of America
Sensation Comics ✷ Wonder Woman
Mickey Mouse ✷ Mickey Mouse
The Flash ✷ Jay Garrick
Adventure Comics ✷ Aquaman
Venus ✷ Venus
Casper The Friendly Ghost ✷ Casper
Strange Adventures ✷ Captain Comet
Donald Duck ✷ Donald Duck
Uncle Scrooge ✷ Uncle Scrooge
Phantom Stranger ✷ Phantom Stranger

# Winners of the Stanley Cup Since You Were Born

The prestigious Stanley Cup has been changing hands since 1893, although the trophy itself has been redesigned more than once. Here are the teams to lift the champagne-filled cup since you were born.

- **Detroit Red Wings (10)**
  1955: 18-year-old Larry Hillman became the youngest player to have his name engraved on the Stanley Cup trophy.

- Chicago Black Hawks (5)
- **Boston Bruins (5)**
  1970: Bobby Orr scored perhaps the most famous goal in NHL history, in midair, to clinch the title.

- **New York Rangers (2)**
  After their 1940 victory, the Rangers would not win another Stanley Cup for another 54 years.

- Toronto Maple Leafs (10)
- Montreal Canadiens (20)
- Philadelphia Flyers (2)
- New York Islanders (4)
- Edmonton Oilers (5)
- **Calgary Flames (1)**
  1989 was the last time a Stanley Cup Final has been played between two teams from Canada.

- Pittsburgh Penguins (5)
- New Jersey Devils (3)
- **Colorado Avalanche (2)**
  1996: A win in their first season after moving from Quebec (where their nickname was the Nordiques).

- Dallas Stars (1)
- Tampa Bay Lightning (3)
- Carolina Hurricanes (1)
- Anaheim Ducks (1)
- Los Angeles Kings (2)
- Washington Capitals (1)
- St. Louis Blues (1)

# On the Silver Screen When You Were 11

From family favorites to the films you weren't allowed to watch, these are the films and actors that drew the praise and the crowds when you turned 11.

An Act of Murder 🎬 Fredric March, Florence Eldridge
Arch of Triumph 🎬 Ingrid Bergman, Charles Laughton
Easter Parade 🎬 Judy Garland, Fred Astaire, Peter Lawford
Force of Evil 🎬 John Garfield, Thomas Gomez, Marie Windsor
**Hamlet** 🎬 Laurence Olivier, Basil Sydney, Eileen Herlie
**Eileen Herlie, who played Olivier's mother, was actually
11 years younger than Olivier.**

The Lady From
Shanghai 🎬 Orson Welles, Rita Hayworth, Everett Sloane
Louisiana Story 🎬 Joseph Boudreaux, Lionel Le Blanc
**Johnny Belinda** 🎬 Jane Wyman, Lew Ayres, Charles Bickford
**The film provoked controversy for its ground-breaking
depiction of rape and the consequences, and was based on
a real-life Prince Edward Island event.**

I Remember Mama 🎬 Irene Dunne, Barbara Bel Geddes
Key Largo 🎬 Humphrey Bogart, Lauren Bacall
The Naked City 🎬 Barry Fitzgerald, Howard Duff, Don Taylor
The Paleface 🎬 Jane Russell, Charles Trowbridge, Jack Searl
Red River 🎬 John Wayne, Montgomery Clift, Joanne Dru
The Red Shoes 🎬 Moira Shearer, Marius Goring, Anton Walbrook
Rope 🎬 Farley Granger, John Dall, Dick Hogan
Sorry, Wrong Number 🎬 Dorothy Neumann, Ann Richards
The Snake Pit 🎬 Olivia de Havilland, Leo Genn, Mark Stevens
Unfaithfully Yours 🎬 Rex Harrison, Rudy Vallee, Linda Darnell
The Treasure of
Sierra Madre 🎬 Tim Holt, Humphrey Bogart
State of the Union 🎬 Katharine Hepburn, Angela Lansbury
The Pirate 🎬 Judy Garland, Gene Kelly, Walter Slezak
A Date with Judy 🎬 Wallace Beery, Jane Powell, Elizabeth Taylor
The Three Musketeers 🎬 Lana Turner, Gene Kelly, June Allyson

# Comic Strips You'll Know

Comic strips took off in the late 19th century and for much of the 20th century they were a dependable feature of everyday life. Some were solo efforts; others became so-called zombie strips, living on well beyond their creator. A century on, some are still going. But how many from your youth will you remember?

| | |
|---|---|
| 1940–52 | The Spirit by Will Eisner |
| 1930– | **Blondie**<br>In 1995, Blondie was one of 20 strips commemorated by the US Postal Service in the Comic Strip Classics series. |
| 1931– | **Dick Tracy**<br>Gould's first idea? A detective called Plainclothes Tracy. |
| 1930–95 | Mickey Mouse |
| 1932– | Mary Worth |
| 1936– | **The Phantom**<br>Lee Falk worked on The Phantom for 63 years and Mandrake The Magician for 65. |
| 1919– | Barney Google and Snuffy Smith |
| 1938– | Nancy |
| 1946– | Mark Trail |
| 1937– | **Prince Valiant**<br>Edward, the Duke of Windsor (previously Edward VIII), called Prince Valiant the "greatest contribution to English literature in the past hundred years." |
| 1934–2003 | **Flash Gordon**<br>Alex Raymond created Flash Gordon to compete with the Buck Rogers comic strip. |
| 1934–77 | Li'l Abner by Al Capp |
| 1925–74 | Etta Kett by Paul Robinson |
| 1947–69 | Grandma by Charles Kuhn |
| 1948– | Rex Morgan, M.D. |
| 1933–87 | Brick Bradford |
| 1950–2000 | **Peanuts by Charles M. Schulz**<br>Schultz was inducted into the Hockey Hall of Fame after building the Redwood Empire Arena near his studio. |
| 1950– | Beetle Bailey |

# Biggest Hits by The King

He may have conquered rock'n'roll, but Elvis's success straddled genres including country music, R&B, and more. These are his Number 1s from across the charts, beginning with the rockabilly "I Forgot…" through the posthumous country hit, "Guitar Man."

I Forgot to Remember to Forget (1955)
Heartbreak Hotel (1956)
I Want You, I Need You, I Love You (1956)
Don't Be Cruel (1956)
Hound Dog (1956)
Love Me Tender (1956)
Too Much (1957)
All Shook Up (1957)
(Let Me Be Your) Teddy Bear (1957)
Jailhouse Rock (1957)
Don't (1957)
Wear My Ring Around Your Neck (1958)
Hard Headed Woman (1958)
A Big Hunk O' Love (1959)
Stuck On You (1960)
It's Now or Never (1960)
Are You Lonesome Tonight? (1960)
Surrender (1961)
Good Luck Charm (1962)
Suspicious Minds (1969)
Moody Blue (1976)
Way Down (1977)
Guitar Man (1981)

# Childhood Candies

In labs across the country, mid-century food scientists dreamed up new and colorful ways to delight children just like you. These are the fruits of their labor, launched before you turned twenty-one.

| | |
|---|---|
| 1945 | Dots (Mason Company) |
| 1946 | Almond Joy (Peter Paul) |
| 1947 | Bazooka Bubble Gum (Topps Candy Company) |
| 1949 | Jolly Rancher (Jolly Rancher Company) |
| 1949 | Junior Mints (James O. Welch Company) |
| 1949 | **Whoppers** (Overland Candy Company)<br>Whoppers were known as "Giants" before 1949. |
| 1949 | Smarties (Ce De Candy, Inc.) |
| 1950 | Cup-O-Gold (Hoffman Candy Company) |
| 1950 | Red Vines (American Licorice Co.) |
| 1950 | Hot Tamales (Just Born) |
| 1950 | Rocky Road Candy Bar (The Annabell Candy Co.) |
| 1952 | Pixy Stix (Sunline, Inc.) |
| 1954 | Atomic Fireballs (Ferrera Candy Co.) |
| 1954 | **Marshmallow Peeps** (Just Born)<br>Today it takes six minutes to make one Peep, but when the candy was first introduced, it took 27 hours! |
| 1954 | Peanut M&Ms (Mars) |
| 1955 | **Chick-O-Sticks** (Atkinson's)<br>These candies were called "Chicken Bones" until they were renamed in 1955. |
| 1950s | Swedish Fish (Malaco) |
| 1950s | Look! Candy Bar (Golden Nugget Candy Co.) |

# Books of the Decade

Ten years of your life that took you from adventure books aged 10 to dense works of profundity at 20—or perhaps just grown-up adventures! How many did you read when they were first published?

| | |
|---|---|
| 1947 | Miracle on 34th Street by Valentine Davies |
| 1948 | The Naked and the Dead by Norman Mailer |
| 1948 | House Divided by Ben Ames Williams |
| 1948 | The Young Lions by Irwin Shaw |
| 1949 | Nineteen Eighty-Four: A Novel by George Orwell |
| 1949 | Point of No Return by John P. Marquand |
| 1950 | I, Robot by Isaac Asimov |
| 1950 | The Cardinal by Henry Morton Robinson |
| 1951 | From Here to Eternity by James Jones |
| 1951 | The Catcher in the Rye by J.D. Salinger |
| 1952 | Invisible Man by Ralph Ellison |
| 1952 | The Old Man and the Sea by Ernest Hemingway |
| 1952 | East of Eden by John Steinbeck |
| 1953 | Fahrenheit 451 by Ray Bradbury |
| 1953 | The Adventures of Augie March by Saul Bellow |
| 1954 | The Fellowship of the Ring by J.R.R. Tolkien |
| 1954 | Under the Net by Iris Murdoch |
| 1955 | Lolita by Vladimir Nabokov |
| 1955 | The Ginger Man by J.P. Donleavy |
| 1955 | The Two Towers by J.R.R. Tolkien |
| 1956 | Peyton Place by Grace Metalious |
| 1956 | Giovanni's Room by James Baldwin |
| 1956 | The Return of the King by J.R.R. Tolkien |

# US Buildings

Some were loathed then, loved now; others, the reverse. Some broke new architectural ground; others housed famous or infamous businesses, or helped to power a nation. All of them were built in your first 18 years.

| | |
|---|---|
| 1937 | San Francisco Mint |
| 1938 | Federal Trade Commission Building |
| 1939 | **Rockefeller Center** |

Between 40,000 and 60,000 workers were employed building the Rockefeller Center. Many came to watch them work from a special viewing shed.

| | |
|---|---|
| 1940 | 10 Rockefeller Plaza |
| 1941 | **Mount Rushmore** |

Fourteen years, a team of 400, a million dollars and a lot of dynamite: Mount Rushmore was unprecedented. The original plan was to model presidents from the waist up.

| | |
|---|---|
| 1942 | New Frontier Hotel and Casino, Las Vegas |
| 1943 | The Pentagon |
| 1944 | Geneva Steel Mill, Utah |
| 1945 | Pacific Gas and Electric Company General Office Building and Annex, SF |
| 1946 | **Flamingo Hotel, Las Vegas** |

The Presidential Suite at The Flamingo originally featured a few extras by request of its mobster owner, "Bugsy" Siegel: bulletproof glass and a secret escape ladder. Siegel was shot dead in Beverly Hills.

| | |
|---|---|
| 1947 | 75 Rockefeller Plaza |
| 1948 | Mile High Stadium, Denver |
| 1949 | Promontory Apartments, Chicago |
| 1950 | Metropolitan Life North Building |
| 1951 | US General Accounting Office Building |
| 1952 | United Nations Secretariat Building |
| 1953 | Sullivan Tower, Nashville |
| 1954 | Republic Center, Dallas |
| 1955 | One Prudential Plaza, Chicago |

# Radio DJs from Your Childhood

If the radio was the soundtrack to your life as you grew up, some of these voices were part of the family. (The stations listed are where these DJs made their name; the dates are their radio broadcasting career).

Wolfman Jack 🎙 XERB/Armed Forces Radio (1960–1995)
Jocko Henderson 🎙 WDAS/W LIB (1952–1991)
**Casey Kasem** 🎙 KRLA (1954–2010)
Kasem was the host of American Top 40 for four decades. By 1986, his show was broadcast on 1,000 radio stations.

Bruce Morrow 🎙 WABC (1959–)
**Murray Kaufman** 🎙 WINS (1958–1975)
You'll likely remember him as Murray the K, the self-declared "fifth Beatle" (he played a lot of music from the Fab Four).

**Alison Steele** 🎙 WNEW-FM (1966–1995)
Aka The Nightbird, Steele was that rarity of the sixties and seventies: a successful female DJ.

**Alan Freed** 🎙 WJW/WINS (1945–1965)
Freed's career crashed after he was found to have been taking payola. His contribution was recognized posthumously when admitted into the Rock n Roll Hall of Fame.

Robert W. Morgan 🎙 KHJ-AM (1955–1998)
Dan Ingram 🎙 WABC (1958–2004)
**Dave Hull** 🎙 KRLA (1955–2010)
Another candidate for the "fifth Beatle," Hull interviewed the band many times.

Hal Jackson 🎙 WBLS (1940–2011)
Johnny Holliday 🎙 KYA (1956–)
**Herb Kent** 🎙 WVON (1944–2016)
"Cool Gent" Herb Kent was the longest-serving DJ on the radio.

Tom Donahue 🎙 WIBG/KYA (1949–1975)
John R. 🎙 WLAC (1941–1973)
Bill Randle 🎙 WERE/WCBS (1940s-2004)
**Jack Spector** 🎙 WMCA (1955–1994)
Spector, one of WMCA's "Good Guys," died on air in 1994. A long silence after playing "I'm in the Mood for Love" alerted station staff.

# It Happened in 1953

Here's a round-up of the most newsworthy events from across the US in the year you turned (sweet) 16.

+ Dr. Jonas Salk announces polio vaccine
+ Ethel and Julius Rosenberg executed for espionage
+ Department of Health, Education, and Welfare created
+ President ends all wage and price control
+ Pilot Chuck Yeager sets new speed record (right)
+ Evidence found linking smoking with cancer
+ New York Yankees win 5th consecutive World Series
+ Supreme Court rules baseball is a sport, not a business
+ Color TVs hit the market
+ Transistor radios go on sale
+ Town renames itself Jim Thorpe
+ Korean War ends
+ Eisenhower inaugurated
+ Earl Warren appointed to Supreme Court
+ Atomic Bomb tourism begins
+ Frozen French fries become available
+ TV dinners offered
+ Hank Williams died
+ Cinemascope used in movies
+ Lucille Ball gives birth to son
+ Matchbox cars introduced
+ Speedbump designed
+ Call sign "Air Force One" created
+ Peeps candy goes on sale

*Born this year:*
- Actress Kim Basinger
- Wrestler Hulk Hogan
- Singer Cyndi Lauper

"America's greatest pilot," Chuck Yeager, was the first to break the speed of sound in 1947. In 1953, Yeager set a new speed record in his Bell X-1A (above), flying at 1650 mph. His test exploits ended with an accident 20 miles high in 1963, but he continued to fly and inspire and train others, rising to the rank of Brigadier General. He died in 2020.

# News Anchors of the Fifties and Sixties

Trusted, familiar, and exclusively male: these are the faces that brought you the news, and the catchphrases they made their own.

**Edward R. Murrow** 📺 CBS (1938-59)
"Good night, and good luck."

**Walter Cronkite** 📺 CBS (1962-81)
"And that's the way it is."

**David Brinkley** 📺 NBC (1956-71)
"Good night, Chet..."

**Chet Huntley** 📺 NBC (1956-70)
"...Good night, David."

Harry Reasoner 📺 CBS & ABC (1961-91)

Frank Reynolds 📺 ABC (1968-70)

**John Charles Daly** 📺 CBS & ABC (1941-60)
"Good night and a good tomorrow."

Douglas Edwards 📺 CBS (1948-62)

Hugh Downs 📺 NBC (1962-71)

John Chancellor 📺 NBC (1970-82)

**Paul Harvey** 📺 ABC Radio (1951-2009)
"Hello Americans, this is Paul Harvey. Stand by for news!"

Mike Wallace 📺 CBS (1963-66)

**John Cameron Swayze** 📺 NBC (1948-56)
"Well, that's the story, folks! This is John Cameron Swayze, and I'm glad we could get together."

Ron Cochran 📺 ABC (1962-65)

Bob Young 📺 ABC (1967-68)

Dave Garroway 📺 NBC (1952-61)

Bill Shadel 📺 ABC (1960-63)

# Fifties Game Shows

It all started so well: appointment radio became appointment TV, with new and crossover game shows bringing us together. But as the decade progressed, the scandal emerged: some shows were fixed. Quiz shows were down, but certainly not out. (Dates include periods off-air.)

Break the Bank 🎙 (1945-57)
Beat The Clock 🎙 (1950-2019)
**Name That Tune** 🏆 (1952-85)
A radio crossover that spawned 25 international versions.

Strike It Rich 🎙 (1947-58)
**The Price Is Right** 🎙 (1956-65)
The original version of the current quiz that began in 1972. This one was hosted by Bill Cullen.

Down You Go 🎙 (1951-56)
I've Got A Secret 🎙 (1952-2006)
What's The Story 🏆 (1951-55)
The $64,000 Question 🎙 (1955-58)
People Are Funny 🏆 (1942-60)
**Tic-Tac-Dough** 🎙 (1956-90)
Early Tic-Tac-Dough contestants were often coached; around three-quarters of the shows in one run were rigged.

The Name's The Same 🎙 (1951-55)
Two For The Money 🎙 (1952-57)
The Big Payoff 🏆 (1951-62)
**Twenty-One** 🎙 (1956-58)
At the heart of the rigging scandal, Twenty-One was the subject of Robert Redford's 1994 movie, Quiz Show.

Masquerade Party 🏆 (1952-60)
**You Bet Your Life** 🏆 (1947-61)
A comedy quiz hosted by Groucho Marx.

**Truth or Consequences** 🎙 (1940-88)
Started life as a radio quiz. TV host Bob Barker signed off with: "Hoping all your consequences are happy ones."

20 Questions 🏆 (1946-55)
What's My Line 🎙 (1950-75)

# Liberty Issue Stamps

First released in 1954, the Liberty Issue drew its name from not one but three depictions of the Statue of Liberty across the denominations. (There was only room for one "real" woman, though.) It coincided with the new era of stamp collecting as a childhood hobby that endured for decades. Were you one of these new miniature philatelists?

**Benjamin Franklin** ½ ¢ Polymath (writer, inventor, scientist)
Franklin discovered the principle of electricity,
the Law of Conservation of Charge.

George Washington 1 ¢ First US President
**Palace of the Governors** 1 ¼ ¢
A building in Santa Fe, New Mexico that served as
the seat of government of New Mexico for centuries.

Mount Vernon 1 ½ ¢ George Washington's plantation
Thomas Jefferson 2 ¢ Polymath; third US President
Bunker Hill Monument 2 ½ ¢ Battle site of the Revolutionary War
Statue of Liberty 3 ¢ Gifted by the people of France
**Abraham Lincoln** 4 ¢ 16th US President
Lincoln received a patent for a flotation device that assisted
boats in moving through shallow water.

The Hermitage 4 ½ ¢ Andrew Jackson's plantation
James Monroe 5 ¢ Fifth US President
Theodore Roosevelt 6 ¢ 26th US President
Woodrow Wilson 7 ¢ 28th US President; served during WW1
John J. Pershing 8 ¢ US Army officer during World War I
Alamo 9 ¢ Site of a pivotal Texas Revolution battle
Independence Hall 10 ¢ Independence declared here
Benjamin Harrison 12 ¢ 23rd US President
John Jay 15 ¢ First Chief Justice of the United States
Monticello 20 ¢ Thomas Jefferson's plantation
Paul Revere 25 ¢ Alerted militia of the British approach
Robert E. Lee 30 ¢ Confederate general in the Civil War
John Marshall 40 ¢ Fourth Chief Justice of the US
Susan B. Anthony 50 ¢ Women's suffrage activist
Patrick Henry $1 Leader of the Dec. of Independence
Alexander Hamilton $5 First Secretary of the Treasury

# The Biggest Hits When You Were 16

The artists that topped the charts when you turned 16 might not be in your top 10 these days, but you'll probably remember them!

Tony Bennett ♪ Rags to Riches
Hank Williams ♪ Your Cheatin' Heart
Les Paul and Mary Ford ♪ Vaya con Dios
Teresa Brewer ♪ Till I Waltz Again with You
Dean Martin ♪ That's Amore
Patti Page ♪ (How Much Is) That Doggie in the Window?
Joni James ♪ Have You Heard?
Eartha Kitt ♪ C'est Si Bon
Nat King Cole ♪ Pretend
Big Mama Thornton ♪ Hound Dog
Frank Sinatra ♪ I've Got the World on a String
Jim Reeves ♪ Mexican Joe
The Davis Sisters ♪ I Forgot More Than You'll Ever Know
Eddie Fisher ♪ With These Hands
Ray Anthony and His Orchestra ♪ Dragnet
Carl Smith ♪ Hey Joe
Ray Charles ♪ Mess Around
Percy Faith and His Orchestra ♪ The Song from Moulin Rouge
Fats Domino ♪ Please Don't Leave Me
Perry Como ♪ Don't Let the Stars Get in Your Eyes
Eddie Fisher ♪ I'm Walking Behind You
The Hilltoppers ♪ P.S. I Love You
Frankie Laine ♪ I Believe
Bill Haley and His Comets ♪ Crazy Man, Crazy

# Medical Advances Before You Were 21

A baby born in 1920 USA had a life expectancy of just 55.4 years. By 2000 that was up to 76.8, thanks to medical advances including many of these.

| | |
|---|---|
| 1937 | Methadone developed |
| 1938 | Ligate procedure (using thread to seal a blood vessel) |
| 1938 | Intramedullary rod (used in fractures) |
| 1940 | Metallic hip replacement |
| 1941 | **Penicillin** |

Years after his discovery of penicillin, Alexander Fleming had been given a tour of a modern, sterile lab. His guide said, "Think of the wonders you would have discovered with a lab like this." He replied, "Not penicillin."

| | |
|---|---|
| 1942 | Mechlorethamine chemotherapy |
| 1943 | Kidney dialysis |
| 1944 | Disposable catheter |
| 1944 | Asperger syndrome (described) |
| 1945 | Oral penicillin |
| 1945 | Amsler grid for eye exam |
| 1946 | All-glass syringe (easier sterilization) |
| 1947 | Defibrillation |
| 1948 | Acetaminophen |
| 1949 | Intraocular lens (myopia and cataracts) |
| 1950 | **Polio vaccine** |

Jonas Salk was asked about taking a patent on the polio vaccine. He replied, "Can you patent the sun?"

| | |
|---|---|
| 1951 | Munchhausen syndrome (described) |
| 1952 | Cloning |
| 1953 | Ultrasound |
| 1954 | Kidney transplant |
| 1955 | Mass immunization of polio |
| 1956 | **Metered-dose inhaler** |

Invented after the teen daughter of head of Riker Labs asked why her asthma medicine couldn't be in a can like hair spray. At the time, asthma medicine was given in ineffective squeeze bulb glass containers.

# Blockbuster Movies When You Were 16

These are the movies that everyone was talking about. How many of them did you see (or have you seen since)?

Peter Pan  Bobby Driscoll, Hans Conried, Kathryn Beaumont
Niagara  Marilyn Monroe, Joseph Cotten, Jean Peters
Shane  Alan Ladd, Jean Arthur, Van Heflin
House of Wax  Vincent Price, Frank Lovejoy, Phyllis Kirk
Pickup on South Street  Richard Widmark, Jean Peters, Thelma Ritter
The Beast from 20,000 Fathoms  Paul Christian, Paula Raymond, Cecil Kellaway
It Came from Outer Space  Charles Drake, Joe Sawyer, Russell Johnson
Gentlemen Prefer Blondes  Marilyn Monroe, Jane Russell
From Here to Eternity  Burt Lancaster, Montgomery Clift, Frank Sinatra
The Robe  Richard Burton, Jean Simmons, Victor Mature
How to Marry a Millionaire  Betty Grable, Marilyn Monroe, Lauren Bacall
Calamity Jane  Doris Day, Howard Keel, Allyn Ann McLerie
**Hondo**  John Wayne, Geraldine Page, Ward Bond
**The filming ran over schedule and director John Farrow left production, leaving John Ford to direct the final scenes.**

House of Wax  Vincent Price, Frank Lovejoy, Phyllis Kirk
**I Confess**  Montgomery Clift, Anne Baxter, Karl Malden
**Director Alfred Hitchcock became frustrated with Montgomery Clift's method acting, having him repeat take after take.**

Julius Caesar  Marlon Brando, James Mason, John Gielgud
The Band Wagon  Fred Astaire, Cyd Charisse, Oscar Levant
Roman Holiday  Gregory Peck, Audrey Hepburn, Eddie Albert
The Wild One  Marlon Brando, Mary Murphy, Robert Keith
The War of the Worlds  Gene Barry, Ann Robinson, Lewis Martin
Stalag 17  William Holden, Otto Preminger, Don Taylor
The Big Heat  Glenn Ford, Gloria Grahame, Jocelyn Brando
Angel Face  Robert Mitchum, Jean Simmons, Mona Freeman

# Game Show Hosts of the Fifties and Sixties

Many of these men were semi-permanent fixtures, their voices and catchphrases ringing through the decades. Some were full-time entertainers; others were on sabbatical from more serious news duties.

John Charles Daly ➤ What's My Line (1950-67)

Art Linkletter ➤ People Are Funny (1943-60)

Garry Moore ➤ I've Got A Secret (1956-64)

Groucho Marx ➤ You Bet Your Life (1949-61)

Warren Hull ➤ Strike It Rich (1947-58)

Herb Shriner ➤ Two For The Money (1952-56)

George DeWitt ➤ Name That Tune (1953-59)

Robert Q. Lewis ➤ Name's The Same (1951-54)

Bill Cullen ➤ The Price Is Right (1956-65)

**Walter Cronkite** ➤ It's News To Me (1954)
"The most trusted man in America" was briefly the host of this topical quiz game. He didn't do it again.

Bill Slater ➤ 20 Questions (1949-52)

Walter Kiernan ➤ Who Said That (1951-54)

Bob Eubanks ➤ The Newlywed Game (1966-74)

Bud Collyer ➤ To Tell The Truth (1956-69)

Jack Barry ➤ Twenty-One (1956-58)

Bert Parks ➤ Break The Bank (1945-57)

Hugh Downs ➤ Concentration (1958-69)

Mike Stokey ➤ Pantomime Quiz (1947-59)

Allen Ludden ➤ Password (1961-75)

**Bob Barker** ➤ Truth or Consequences (1956-74)
Barker also spent 35 years hosting The Price Is Right.

Hal March ➤ $64,000 Question (1955-58)

**Monty Hall** ➤ Let's Make A Deal (1963-91)
Monty—born "Monte", but misspelled on an early publicity photo—was also a philanthropist who raised around $1 billion over his lifetime.

Johnny Carson ➤ Who Do You Trust? (1957-63)

# Kitchen Inventions

The 20th-century kitchen was a playground for food scientists and engineers with new labor-saving devices and culinary shortcuts launched every year. These all made their debut before you were 18.

| | |
|---|---|
| 1937 | Waring blender |
| 1938 | Formica countertop |
| 1939 | Twist tie |
| 1939 | Old Bay seasoning |
| 1940 | Dishwasher with drying element |
| 1941 | Trash compactor |
| 1942 | Vlasic pickles |
| 1943 | Uncle Ben's rice |
| 1944 | Dish drying cabinet |
| 1945 | Minute Maid orange concentrate |
| 1946 | Food processor |
| 1946 | Tupperware products |
| 1947 | Zen Rex speed peeler |
| 1948 | Aluminum foil |
| 1949 | **Reddi-Wip cream** |

**Reddi-Wip** has been chosen as one of The Top 100 consumer inventions of 20th century and made its inventor, Aaron Lapin, the 'Whipped Cream King', millions of dollars.

| | |
|---|---|
| 1950 | Green Garbage Bags |
| 1951 | Kenwood food mixer |
| 1952 | Automatic coffee pot |
| 1952 | Bread clip |
| 1953 | Combination washer-dryer |
| 1954 | Zipper storage bag |

# Around the World When You Turned 18

These are the headlines from around the globe as you were catapulted into adulthood.

+ West Germany joins NATO
+ Soviet battleship explodes
+ Baghdad Pact is signed
+ Winter storms devastate England
+ Sudan Civil War starts
+ Princess Margaret cancels wedding plans
+ Austria declares its permanent neutrality
+ Cyprus declares state of emergency
+ Strikers in London delay newspapers for a month
+ Lolita published
+ Soviets discover diamond mine
+ Railroad workers strike in UK
+ Commercial TV station airs advertisements
+ Riots in Montreal over hockey team decision
+ Warsaw Pact is signed
+ Churchill resigns as prime minister
+ Ferry sinks off Japan's coast, killing over 150
+ Soviet sub launches ballistic missile
+ Soviet army leaves Austria
+ Organization of Central American States meets
+ Tragedy occurs at Le Mans
+ Juan Peron overthrown by military
+ St. Lawrence Seaway opens
+ War breaks out in Vietnam
+ New government forms in Turkey

# Super Bowl Champions Since You Were Born

These are the teams that have held a 7-pound, sterling silver Vince Lombardi trophy aloft during the Super Bowl era, and the number of times they've done it in your lifetime.

- **New England Patriots (6)**
  2001: The Super Bowl MVP, Tom Brady, had been a 6th round draft pick in 2000.
- Pittsburgh Steelers (6)
- Dallas Cowboys (5)
- San Francisco 49ers (5)
- **Green Bay Packers (4)**
  1967: To gain a berth in the Super Bowl, the Packers defeated the Dallas Cowboys in The Ice Bowl at 15 degrees below zero.
- New York Giants (4)
- **Denver Broncos (3)**
  2015: After the Broncos won their first Super Bowl 18 years prior, Broncos owner Pat Bowlen dedicated the victory to long-time quarterback John Elway ("This one's for John!"). After the 2015 victory, John Elway (now general manager) dedicated it to the ailing Bowlen ("This one's for Pat!").
- Washington Football Team (3)
- Las Vegas Raiders (3)
- Miami Dolphins (2)
- Indianapolis Colts (2)
- Kansas City Chiefs (2)
- Baltimore Ravens (2)
- Tampa Bay Buccaneers (2)
- **St. Louis/Los Angeles Rams (2)**
  1999: The Rams were led to the Super Bowl by Kurt Warner, who had been a grocery store clerk after college.
- Seattle Seahawks (1)
- Philadelphia Eagles (1)
- **Chicago Bears (1)**
  The 1985 Bears are known for their song, The Super Bowl Shuffle.
- New York Jets (1)
- New Orleans Saints (1)

# Across the Nation

**18**

Voting. Joining the military. Turning 18 is serious stuff. Here's what everyone was reading about in the year you reached this milestone.

- Actor James Dean killed
- Bomb destroys airliner over Colorado
- Albert Einstein died
- Hurricane Diane hits the northeast
- Disneyland opens
- Marlboro cowboy rides onto the scene
- Rosa Parks refuses to change seats (right)
- Author William Faulkner wins Pulitzer Prize
- Tonka trucks introduced
- School bus hit by freight train
- Jonas Salk explains why he will not patent polio vaccine
- Brooklyn Dodgers win World Series
- Emmett Till murdered
- Jim Henson (and friend) perform on local television
- Quaker Oats sells deeds to land in Yukon Territory
- U-2 plane takes flight
- Pentagon announces plans for ICBMs
- Minimum wage raised to $1.00
- Montgomery bus boycott sparks civil rights movement
- Roy Kroc opens the first McDonald's franchise
- Singer Marian Anderson performs at the Met
- Actress Lee Meriwether becomes Miss America

*Born this year:*
- Microsoft's Bill Gates
- Apple's Steve Jobs
- Actor Bruce Willis
- Actress Whoopi Goldberg

Rosa Parks had been fighting racism long before December 1955, when James F. Blake ordered Parks and three others to give up their seats and move to the back. She knew of the plans for a bus boycott. She'd even had a previous run-in with Blake: 12 years before, she'd entered his bus by the "wrong" door. Her refusal to move in 1955 because she was "tired of giving in" led to her arrest and triggered the long-anticipated and successful boycott.

But that arrest is not the moment photographed here. Three months later, arrest warrants were issued for around 90 leaders, including Parks, for the financial harm they were causing to the bus company. They dressed up smartly before turning themselves in, knowing this to be another step on the march toward equality.

# US Open Champions

Winners while you were between the ages of the youngest (John McDermott, 1911, 19 years) and the oldest (Hale Irwin, 1990, at 45). Planning a win? Better hurry up!

| | |
|---|---|
| 1956 | Cary Middlecoff |
| 1957 | **Dick Mayer** |

This year, Jack Nicklaus started the first of his record 44 consecutive starts (1957–2000).

| | |
|---|---|
| 1958 | Tommy Bolt |
| 1959 | Billy Casper |
| 1960 | **Arnold Palmer** |

Palmer set a record by coming back from seven strokes down in the final round to win the title.

| | |
|---|---|
| 1961 | Gene Littler |
| 1962 | Jack Nicklaus |
| 1963 | Julius Boros |
| 1964 | Ken Venturi |
| 1965 | Gary Player |
| 1966 | Billy Casper |
| 1967 | Jack Nicklaus |
| 1968 | Lee Trevino |
| 1969 | Orville Moody |
| 1970 | Tony Jacklin |
| 1971 | Lee Trevino |
| 1972 | Jack Nicklaus |
| 1973 | Johnny Miller |
| 1974 | Hale Irwin |
| 1975 | Lou Graham |
| 1976 | Jerry Pate |
| 1977 | Hubert Green |
| 1978 | Andy North |
| 1979 | Hale Irwin |
| 1980 | **Jack Nicklaus** |

Nicklaus set the record for years (18) between the first and last US Open victory.

| | |
|---|---|
| 1981 | David Graham |
| 1982 | Tom Watson |

# Popular Girls' Names

**20**

If you started a family at a young age, these are the names you're most likely to have chosen. And even if you didn't pick them, a lot of Americans did!

Mary

**Susan**
1957 marked the start of a four-year run in second position for Susan, though she could never quite claim the top spot.

Linda

Debra

Karen

Deborah

**Cynthia**
Seventh place for Cynthia: her best ever ranking.

Patricia

Barbara

Donna

Nancy

Pamela

Brenda

Sharon

Sandra

Cheryl

Diane

Carol

Cindy

Kathy

Kathleen

Elizabeth

Janet

Teresa

Denise

**Rising and falling stars:**
Annette and Jill graced the Top 100 for the first time; for Elaine and Marie it would be their last ever year in the spotlight.

# Animals Extinct in Your Lifetime

Billions of passenger pigeons once flew the US skies. By 1914, they had been trapped to extinction. Not every species dies at our hands, but it's a sobering roll-call. (Date is year last known alive or declared extinct).

| | |
|---|---|
| 1939 | Toolache wallaby |
| 1940 | Javan lapwing |
| 1943 | Desert bandicoot |
| 1951 | Yemen gazelle |
| 1952 | **Deepwater cisco fish** <br> Once found in Lake Huron and Michigan, ciscoes were overfished and crowded out by invasive parasites and alewife herring. Result? Extinction. |
| 1960 | Candango mouse, Brasilia |
| 1962 | Red-bellied opossum, Argentina |
| 1963 | Kākāwahie honeycreeper, Hawaii |
| 1964 | South Island snipe, New Zealand |
| 1967 | **Yellow blossom pearly mussel** <br> Habitat loss and pollution proved terminal for this Tennessee resident. |
| 1968 | Mariana fruit bat (Guam) |
| 1971 | Lake Pedder earthworm, Tasmania |
| 1972 | Bushwren, New Zealand |
| 1977 | Siamese flat-barbelled catfish, Thailand |
| 1979 | Yunnan Lake newt, China |
| 1981 | Southern gastric-brooding frog, Australia |
| 1986 | Las Vegas dace |
| 1989 | Golden toad (see right) |
| 1990 | Dusky seaside sparrow, East Coast USA |
| 2000 | **Pyrenean ibex, Iberia** <br> In 2003 this species was brought back to life through cloning. Sadly the newborn ibex died. |
| 2001 | Caspian tiger, Central Asia |
| 2012 | **Pinta giant tortoise** <br> The rarest creature in the world for the latter half of his 100-year life, Lonesome George of the Galapagos was the last remaining Pinta tortoise. |

The observed history of the golden toad is brief, and tragic. It wasn't discovered until 1964, abundant in a pristine area of Costa Rica. By 1989 it had gone, a victim of rising temperatures.

# Popular Boys' Names

Here are the top boys' names for this year. Many of the most popular choices haven't shifted much since you were born, but more modern names are creeping in…

**Michael**
For 44 years from 1954 onwards, Michael was the nation's most popular name. (There was one blip in 1960 when David came first.)

James
David
Robert
John
William
Mark
Richard
Thomas
Steven
Charles
Joseph
Gary
Kenneth
Donald
Daniel
Ronald
Paul
Timothy
Kevin
Jeffrey
Larry
Gregory
Stephen
Edward
Brian

**Rising and falling stars:**
Eugene, Leonard, Frederick and Harry were all heading for the door; Jeff was the only new face in the Top 100 this year.

# Popular Movies When You Were 21

The biggest stars in the biggest movies: these are the films the nation were enjoying as you entered into adulthood.

Gigi  Leslie Caron, Louis Jourdan, Maurice Chevalier
**South Pacific**  Rossano Brazzi, Mitzi Gaynor, John Kerr
The soundtrack was #1 on the Billboard 200 in the US for seven months, the fourth longest run ever.

Marjorie Morningstar  Gene Kelly, Natalie Wood, Claire Trevor
Vertigo  James Stewart, Kim Novak, Tom Helmore
Touch of Evil  Charlton Heston, Janet Leigh, Joseph Calleia
The Bravados  Gregory Peck, Lee Van Cleef, Stephen Boyd
Indiscreet  Cary Grant, Ingrid Bergman, Cecil Parker
The Big Country  Gregory Peck, Jean Simmons, Charlton Heston
**Cat on a Hot Tin Roof**  Elizabeth Taylor, Paul Newman, Burl Ives
A week into production, Elizabeth Taylor contracted a virus that caused her to cancel plans to fly to New York where her husband was to receive an honor. The plane crashed.

I Want to Live!  Susan Hayward, Simon Oakland
The Inn of the
Sixth Happiness  Ingrid Bergman, Curt Jurgens, Robert Donat
Auntie Mame  Rosalind Russell, Forrest Tucker, Coral Browne
Separate Tables  Rita Hayworth, Deborah Kerr, David Niven
The Defiant Ones  Tony Curtis, Sidney Poitier, Theodore Bikel
Some Came Running  Frank Sinatra, Dean Martin, Shirley MacLaine
Man of the West  Gary Cooper, Julie London, Lee J. Cobb
Horror of Dracula  Peter Cushing, Michael Gough, Melissa Stribling
The Vikings  Kirk Douglas, Tony Curtis, Janet Leigh
Windjammer (doc.)  Niels Arntsen, Erik Bye, Pablo Casals
Run Silent Run Deep  Burt Lancaster, Clark Gable, Jack Warden
King Creole  Elvis Presley, Carolyn Jones, Walter Matthau
The Blob  Steve McQueen, Earl Rowe, Aneta Corsaut

# Across the Nation

A selection of national headlines from the year you turned 21. But how many can you remember?

+ Flag with 50 stars designed by junior high student
+ Singer Jerry Lee Lewis sparks controversy with marriage to child relative
+ Charles Starkweather goes on a killing spree
+ Radio's "Payola" scandal breaks
+ Actress Lana Turner's boyfriend killed by her teenage daughter in justifiable homicide
+ Frank Lloyd Wright designs his only gas station project
+ Record-setting tsunami hits Alaska
+ Worst ever school bus tragedy kills 26 in Kentucky
+ American Express card introduced
+ Superglue sold
+ Hula Hoops hit the market
+ "Look Ma, no cavities!" ad created
+ Bank of America begins a program that becomes the Visa Card
+ Crayola renames Prussian Blue to Midnight Blue
+ Mr. Clean gets to work
+ Candy necklaces go on sale
+ Pizza Hut founded
+ New York Yankees win the World Series
+ Last battleship decommissioned
+ Vanguard I satellite launched
+ Two servicemen are laid in the Tomb of the Unknown Soldiers
+ Singer Elvis Presley inducted into the US Army (right)

*Born this year:*
ᛞ Singers Prince, Madonna, and Michael Jackson
ᛞ Actor Kevin Bacon
ᛞ Rapper Ice T

In 1958, many parents and teachers, long concerned about the pernicious effect of rock'n'roll, sighed with relief. Elvis would serve as a regular soldier. Behind the scenes, the singer's agent gave him little choice. Joining the Special Services—an option that would have seen Elvis avoid service in return for concerts—meant giving away worldwide royalties, and wouldn't prove popular with the public in any case. He was in a "funny position," as he would later say. His fate was sealed, and on March 24, he reported for duty.

Elvis's early army life was scarred by homesickness and the death of his mother, aged 46, from a heart attack. The following month, Elvis was posted to West Germany to complete his draft.

# The Biggest Hits
# When You Were 21

The artists you love at 21 are with you for life.
How many of these hits from this milestone
year can you still hum or sing in the tub?

Chuck Berry ♪ Johnny B. Goode
Sheb Wooley ♪ Purple People Eater
Little Richard ♪ Good Golly, Miss Molly
Perry Como ♪ Catch a Falling Star
The Chantels ♪ Maybe
Ritchie Valens ♪ La Bamba
The Everly Brothers ♪ All I Have to Do Is Dream
Conway Twitty ♪ It's Only Make Believe
The Coasters ♪ Yakety Yak
The Monotones ♪ Book of Love
Johnny Cash ♪ Guess Things Happen That Way
Bobby Day ♪ Rockin' Robin
The Silhouettes ♪ Get a Job
Perez Prado and His Orchestra ♪ Patricia
The Kingston Trio ♪ Tom Dooley
Bobby Darin ♪ Splish Splash
The Teddy Bears ♪ To Know Him Is to Love Him
Marty Robbins ♪ The Story of My Life
Big Bopper ♪ Chantilly Lace
The Champs ♪ Tequila
The McGuire Sisters ♪ Sugartime
Sam Cooke ♪ I'll Come Running Back to You
The Crests ♪ Sixteen Candles
The Platters ♪ Twilight Time

# Popular Food in the 1960s

Changes in society didn't stop at the front door: a revolution in the kitchen brought us exotic new recipes, convenience in a can, and even space-age fruit flavors. These are the tastes of a decade, but how many of them were on the menu for your family?

**McDonald's Big Mac**
First served in 1967 by a Pittsburgh franchisee.
Royal Shake-a-Pudd'n Dessert Mix
Tunnel of Fudge Cake
Campbell's SpaghettiOs
Pop-Tarts
B&M's canned bread
**Cool Whip**
A time-saving delight that originally contained no milk or cream, meaning that it could be frozen and transported easily.

Grasshopper pie
Beech-Nut Fruit Stripe Gum
Sandwich Loaf
**Lipton Onion Soup Dip**
Millions of packets are still sold each year of this favorite that was once known as "Californian Dip".

Jello salad
Hires Root Beer
Baked Alaska
**Tang**
Invented by William A. Mitchell who also concocted Cool Whip, Tang was used by astronauts to flavor the otherwise unpalatable water on board the Gemini and Apollo missions.

Corn Diggers
Teem soda
Eggo Waffles
Kraft Shake 'N Bake
**Maypo oatmeal**
In 1985, Dire Straights sang, "I want my MTV"—an echo of the stars who'd shouted the same words to promote the new station. But 30 years before that (and the inspiration for MTV's campaign), an animated child yelled, "I want my Maypo!"

# Fashion in the Sixties

As a child, you (generally) wear what you're given. It's only in hindsight, on fading Polaroids, that you recognize that your outfits carried the fashion imprint of the day. Whether you were old or bold enough to carry off a pair of bell bottoms, though, is a secret that should remain between you and your photo albums.

**Bell bottoms**
Bell bottoms were widely available at Navy surplus and thrift stores at a time when second-hand shopping was on the rise.

Miniskirts and mini dresses

Peasant blouses

**Rudi Gernreich**
Pope Paul IV banned Catholics from wearing his monokini–
a topless swim suit.

US flag clothing

Tulle turbans

Shift dresses

**Collarless jackets**
This jacket trend was popularized by the Beatles in 1963.

Babydoll dresses

V-neck tennis sweaters

Afghan coats

**Leopard print clothing**
In 1962, Jackie Kennedy wore a leopard print coat which caused a spike in demand for leopard skin, leading to the death of up to 250,000 leopards. The coat's designer, Oleg Cassini, felt guilty about it for the rest of his life.

Tie-dye clothing

Short, brightly colored, shapeless dresses

Pillbox hats

Mary Quant

Maxi skirts

Bonnie Cashin

Plaid

Poor boy sweaters

Pea coats

# Around the World When You Turned 25

With the growing reach of news organizations, events from outside our borders were sometimes front-page news. How many do you remember?

✦ Burundi claims independence from Belgium
✦ Man shot on Berlin Wall, left to die
✦ Floods around Hamburg kill 300
✦ Jamaica becomes independent
✦ Britain and France develop the Concorde
✦ 300 people use a tunnel to escape Berlin
✦ France grants Algeria independence
✦ Train crash in Denmark kills 93
✦ Nehru becomes Indian PM
✦ Hundreds die in avalanche in Peru
✦ Brazil wins World Cup
✦ Rolling Stones perform in public
✦ Pope John XXIII excommunicates Castro
✦ Tokyo triple-train crash kills 160
✦ Gay Byrnes begins broadcasting
✦ Eichmann is hanged for war crimes
✦ Plane crashes in Paris
✦ Rwanda splits from Burundi and gains independence
✦ French Foreign Legion leaves Algeria
✦ Cuban Missile Crisis grips the world's attention
✦ Argentine woman crowned Miss Universe
✦ Soviets agree to send arms to Cuba
✦ East Germany restarts conscription
✦ Military coup overthrows government in Burma
✦ Algeria joins the Arab League

# Cars of the 1960s

Smaller cars. More powerful cars. More distinctive cars. More variety, yes: but the success of imported models such as the Volkswagen Beetle was a sign that more fundamental changes lay ahead for The Big Three.

| | |
|---|---|
| 1940 | Ford Lincoln Continental |
| 1949 | Volkswagen Beetle |
| 1950 | Volkswagen Type 2 (Microbus) |
| 1958 | **General Motors Chevrolet Impala**<br>In 1965, the Impala sold more than 1 million units, the most sold by any model in the US since WWII. |
| 1958 | American Motors Corporation Rambler Ambassador |
| 1959 | General Motors Chevrolet El Camino |
| 1959 | Ford Galaxie |
| 1960 | **Ford Falcon**<br>The cartoon strip "Peanuts" was animated for TV to market the Falcon. |
| 1960 | General Motors Pontiac Tempest |
| 1960 | General Motors Chevrolet Corvair |
| 1961 | **Jaguar E-Type**<br>Ranked first in The Daily Telegraph UK's list of the world's "100 most beautiful cars" of all time. |
| 1961 | Chrysler Newport |
| 1962 | Shelby Cobra |
| 1963 | General Motors Buick Riviera |
| 1963 | Porsche 911 |
| 1963 | Kaiser-Jeep Jeep Wagoneer |
| 1964 | **Ford Mustang**<br>The song of the same name reached #6 on the R&B Charts in 1966. That year, more Ford Mustangs were sold (550,000) than any other car. |
| 1964 | General Motors Chevrolet Chevelle |
| 1964 | Chrysler Plymouth Barracuda |
| 1964 | General Motors Pontiac GTO |
| 1967 | General Motors Chevrolet Camaro |
| 1967 | Ford Mercury Cougar |
| 1968 | Chrysler Plymouth Road Runner |

# Books of the Decade

Were you a voracious bookworm in your twenties? Or a more reluctant reader, only drawn by the biggest titles of the day? Here are the new titles that fought for your attention.

| | |
|---|---|
| 1957 | On the Road by Jack Kerouac |
| 1957 | Atlas Shrugged by Ayn Rand |
| 1958 | Breakfast at Tiffany's by Truman Capote |
| 1958 | Doctor Zhivago by Boris Pasternak |
| 1958 | Exodus by Leon Uris |
| 1959 | The Haunting of Hill House by Shirley Jackson |
| 1959 | Naked Lunch by William S. Burroughs |
| 1959 | Advise and Consent by Allen Drury |
| 1960 | To Kill a Mockingbird by Harper Lee |
| 1960 | Hawaii by James Michener |
| 1961 | Catch-22 by Joseph Heller |
| 1961 | Stranger in a Strange Land by Robert A. Heinlein |
| 1962 | One Flew Over the Cuckoo's Nest by Ken Kesey |
| 1962 | Franny and Zooey by J.D. Salinger |
| 1963 | The Bell Jar by Sylvia Plath |
| 1963 | The Feminine Mystique by Betty Friedan |
| 1963 | A Clockwork Orange by Anthony Burgess |
| 1964 | The Group by Mary McCarthy |
| 1964 | Herzog by Saul Bellow |
| 1964 | The Spy Who Came in from the Cold by John le Carré |
| 1964 | Up the Down Staircase by Bel Kaufman |
| 1965 | Dune by Frank Herbert |
| 1966 | Valley of the Dolls by Jacqueline Susann |
| 1966 | In Cold Blood by Truman Capote |

# Prominent Americans

This new set of definitive stamps, issued from 1965 onwards, aimed to do a better job of capturing the diversity of the Americans who made a nation. The series doubled the previous number of women depicted…to two. How many did you have in your collection?

Thomas Jefferson 1 ¢ 🖼 Third US President
Albert Gallatin 1 ¼ ¢ 🖼 Fourth Treasury Secretary
Frank Lloyd Wright 2 ¢ 🖼 Architect
Francis Parkman 3 ¢ 🖼 Historian
Abraham Lincoln 4 ¢ 🖼 16th US President
George Washington 5 ¢ 🖼 First US President
Franklin D Roosevelt 6 ¢ 🖼 32nd US President
**Dwight Eisenhower** 6 / 8 ¢ 🖼 34th US President
In 1957, Eisenhower became the first president to travel by helicopter instead of a limo, en route to Camp David (which he had called Shangri-La, but renamed after his grandson).

Benjamin Franklin 7 ¢ 🖼 Polymath
Albert Einstein 8 ¢ 🖼 Physicist
Andrew Jackson 10 ¢ 🖼 7th US President
Henry Ford 12 ¢ 🖼 Founder of Ford Motor Company
John F. Kennedy 13 ¢ 🖼 35th US President
**Fiorello LaGuardia** 14 ¢ 🖼 Mayor of New York City in WWII
**Read Dick Tracy comics on the radio during a paper strike.**

Oliver Wendell Holmes, Jr 15 ¢ 🖼 Supreme Court Justice
Ernie Pyle 16 ¢ 🖼 Journalist during World War II
**Elizabeth Blackwell** 18 ¢ 🖼 First woman to get a medical degree.
After 11 college rejections, male students at Geneva Medical College all voted for her acceptance. They did it as a joke.

George C Marshall 20 ¢ 🖼 Sec. of State and Sec. of Defense
Amadeo Giannini 21 ¢ 🖼 Founder of Bank of America
Frederick Douglass 25 ¢ 🖼 Slavery escapee,abolitionist leader
John Dewey 30 ¢ 🖼 Educational pioneer
Thomas Paine 40 ¢ 🖼 Helped inspire the American Revolution
Lucy Stone 50 ¢ 🖼 Suffragist and slavery campaigner
Eugene O'Neill $1 🖼 Playwright
John Bassett Moore $5 🖼 Jurist

# Sixties Game Shows

Recovery from the quiz show scandal of the fifties was a gradual process. Big prize money was out; games were in—the sillier the better, or centered around relationships. "Popcorn for the mind," as game show creator Chuck Barris memorably put it.

College Bowl 🏆 (1953-70)
Snap Judgment 🏆 (1967-69)
To Tell The Truth 🏆 (1956-present)
Dough Re Mi 🏆 (1958-60)
Camouflage 🏆 (1961-62 & 1980)
Dream House 🏆 (1968-84)
Say When!! 🏆 (1961-65)
**Let's Make A Deal** 🏆 (1963-present)
The long-time presenter of the show, Monty Hall, gave rise to the eponymous problem: when one door in three hides a prize and you've made your pick, should you change your answer when the host reveals a "zonk" (dud) behind another door? (The counterintuitive answer is yes!)

Your First Impression 🏆 (1962-64)
**Supermarket Sweep** 🏆 (1965-present)
In one of its many comebacks, 1990 episodes of Supermarket Sweep featured monsters roaming the aisles including Frankenstein and Mr. Yuk.

You Don't Say! 🏆 1963-79)
It's Your Bet 🏆 (1969-73)
Yours For A Song 🏆 (1961-63)
Concentration 🏆 (1958-91)
Seven Keys 🏆 (1960-65)
Queen For A Day 🏆 1945-1970)
Password 🏆 (1961-75)
Video Village 🏆 (1960-62)
**Who Do You Trust?** 🏆 (1957-63)
Originally titled, "Do You Trust Your Wife?"
Personality 🏆 (1967-69)
Beat The Odds 🏆 (1961-69)

# Across the Nation

**30** Another decade passes and you're well into adulthood. Were you reading the news, or making it? Here are the national stories that dominated the front pages.

- ✦ Thurgood Marshall sworn into the Supreme Court
- ✦ Stalin's daughter defects to US
- ✦ Battleship (the game) sets sail
- ✦ Maytag repairman becomes the loneliest guy
- ✦ Handheld calculator invented
- ✦ 7-11 Slurpees offered nationwide
- ✦ Green Bay Packers win Super Bowl
- ✦ Saint Louis Cardinals win World Series
- ✦ Astronauts die in Apollo launchpad fire
- ✦ Twenty-Fifth Amendment ratified
- ✦ Human Be-in begins the "Summer of Love"
- ✦ Muhammad Ali refuses military service
- ✦ Martin Luther King Jr. speaks out against the Vietnam War
- ✦ Tornadoes strike Midwest
- ✦ Supreme Court decides Loving v. Virginia
- ✦ Freedom of Information Act goes into effect
- ✦ Riots in Detroit and other cities increase (right)
- ✦ Future senator John McCain shot down as a navy pilot
- ✦ Vietnam protest march on the Pentagon
- ✦ Apollo 4 test spacecraft launched
- ✦ Big Mac introduced locally, then nationally
- ✦ Corporation for Public Broadcasting founded
- ✦ National Transportation Safety Board (NTSB) created
- ✦ JFK's eternal flame lit at Arlington National Cemetery

*Born this year:*
- ௸ Actor Matt LeBlanc
- ௸ Actress Julia Roberts
- ௸ Talk show host Jimmy Kimmel

July 1967: of the many race riots over the course of that summer, few were as intense or long-lived as the disturbances in Detroit. For five days, fires were set and stores looted. The National Guard and US Army Airborne divisions were called in to quell the violence; 43 died, and damage ran to tens of millions of dollars.

# The Biggest Hits When You Were 30...

How many of these big tunes from the year you turned thirty will still strike a chord decades later?

Frankie Valli 🎸 Can't Take My Eyes Off
Loretta Lynn 🎸 Don't Come Home A' Drinkin'
(With Lovin' on Your Mind)
Procol Harum 🎸 A White Shade of Pale
The Box Tops 🎸 The Letter
The Turtles 🎸 Happy Together
Aretha Franklin 🎸 Respect
The Rolling Stones 🎸 Let's Spend
the Night Together
Glen Campbell 🎸 Gentle on My Mind
Johnny Cash and June Carter 🎸 Jackson
Sam & Dave 🎸 Soul Man
Diana Ross and the Supremes 🎸 Reflections
The Spencer Davis Group 🎸 Gimme Some Lovin'
Tammy Wynette 🎸 I Don't Want to Play House
The Who 🎸 I Can See for Miles
Van Morrison 🎸 Brown Eyed Girl
Jimi Hendrix 🎸 Hey Joe
The Young Rascals 🎸 Groovin'
Stevie Wonder 🎸 I Was Made to Love Her
Sonny and Cher 🎸 And the Beat Goes On
Marvin Gaye and Tammi Terrell 🎸 Ain't No Mountain
High Enough
Aaron Neville 🎸 Tell It Like It Is
Dionne Warwick 🎸 I Say a Little Prayer
The Beatles 🎸 All You Need Is Love
The Doors 🎸 Light My Fire

# ...and the Movies You Saw That Year, Too

From award winners to crowd pleasers, here are the movies that played as your third decade drew to a close.

El Dorado 🎟 John Wayne, Robert Mitchum, James Caan
**The Jungle Book** 🎟 Phil Harris, Sebastian Cabot, George Sanders
**The Beatles were planned to appear, but John Lennon
refused to work on animated films.**

In the Heat of the Night 🎟 Sidney Poitier, Rod Steiger, Lee Grant
Valley of the Dolls 🎟 Barbara Parkins, Patty Duke, Sharon Tate
In Like Flint 🎟 James Coburn, Lee J. Cobb, Jerry Goldsmith
Divorce American Style 🎟 Dick Van Dyke, Debbie Reynolds, Jason Robards
Guess Who's
Coming to Dinner 🎟 Spencer Tracy, Sidney Poitier, Katharine Hepburn
The Born Losers 🎟 Tom Laughlin, Elizabeth James, Jeremy Slate
Doctor Dolittle 🎟 Rex Harrison, Samantha Eggar, Anthony Newley
Dirty Dozen 🎟 Lee Marvin, Ernest Borgnine, Jim Brown
The Graduate 🎟 Dustin Hoffman, Anne Bancroft, Katharine Ross
The War Wagon 🎟 John Wayne, Kirk Douglas, Howard Keel
The Taming
of the Shrew 🎟 Elizabeth Taylor, Richard Burton, Natasha Pyne
In Cold Blood 🎟 Robert Blake, Scott Wilson, John Forsythe
Hombre 🎟 Paul Newman, Frederic March, Richard Boone
Thoroughly
Modern Millie 🎟 Julie Andrews, Mary Tyler Moore, James Fox
Wait Until Dark 🎟 Audrey Hepburn, Alan Arkin, Richard Crenna
Casino Royale 🎟 Peter Sellers, Ursula Andress, Barbara Bouchet
Camelot 🎟 Richard Harris, Vanessa Redgrave, Franco Nero
The Ambushers 🎟 Dean Martin, Senta Berger, Janice Rule
Cool Hand Luke 🎟 Paul Newman, George Kennedy, J.D. Cannon
Bonnie and Clyde 🎟 Warren Beatty, Faye Dunaway
**To Sir With Love** 🎟 Sidney Poitier, Christian Roberts, Judy Geeson
**The film's title song was the best-selling single in the
United States in 1967.**

You Only Live Twice 🎟 Sean Connery, Akiko Wakabayashi, Mie Hama

# Around the House

Sometimes with a fanfare but often by stealth, inventions and innovations transformed the 20th-century household. Here's what arrived between the ages of 10 and 30.

| | |
|---|---|
| 1947 | Ajax cleaning powder |
| 1948 | Polaroid camera |
| 1949 | 45-rpm record |
| 1950 | Bactine antiseptic |
| 1951 | Super glue |
| 1952 | Frosted Flakes cereal |
| 1953 | **WD-40 spray** |

**WD-40 spray**
Now a household essential, "Water Displacement 40th Formula" was created for the aerospace industry to protect, clean, and lubricate—much as it is now used by everyone else.

| | |
|---|---|
| 1954 | Rolaids calcium tablets |
| 1955 | TV remote control |
| 1956 | Snooze alarm clock |
| 1956 | Yahtzee board game |
| 1956 | Velcro |
| 1957 | Off mosquito repellent |
| 1958 | Friskies cat food |
| 1959 | Princess line telephone |
| 1960 | Downy fabric softener |
| 1961 | Head & Shoulders shampoo |
| 1962 | Arco lamp |
| 1963 | **Chips Ahoy! chocolate chip cookies** |

**Chips Ahoy! chocolate chip cookies**
An elementary teacher and her class wrote Nabisco saying that they did not find 1000 chips, as stated on the bag. Nabisco flew a rep to their school and demonstrated to the students (and the media) how to find all the chips.

| | |
|---|---|
| 1963 | Push button Touchtone phone |
| 1963 | Lava lamps |
| 1964 | Portable TVs |
| 1964 | Sharpie permanent markers |
| 1965 | Cordless telephone |

*Mary Evans / Everett Collection*

Here's one that didn't quite make the grade: AT&T's Picturephone, demonstrated here at the 1964 New York World's Fair. A trial set up that year invited the public to rent two of the Picturephone rooms set up in New York, Chicago, and Washington ($16 for 3 minutes). The take-up over the following years was almost nil, but Picturephones went on sale in 1970 anyway with a prediction of a billion-dollar business by 1980. The devices were withdrawn from sale in 1973.

# Female Olympic Gold Medalists in Your Lifetime

These are the women who have stood atop the podium the greatest number of times at the Summer Olympics, whether in individual or team events.

**Jenny Thompson** (8) ♂ Swimming
Thompson is an anesthesiologist. She started her medical training in 2000–although she took time out while studying to win further gold World Championship medals.

Katie Ledecky (7) ♂ Swimming
Allyson Felix (7) ♂ Athletics
Amy Van Dyken (6) ♂ Swimming
Dana Vollmer (5) ♂ Swimming
Missy Franklin (5) ♂ Swimming
Sue Bird (5) ♂ Basketball
**Diana Taurasi** (5) ♂ Basketball
The late Kobe Bryant dubbed Taurasi the "white mamba"; for others she is the G.O.A.T. in women's basketball.

Allison Schmitt (4) ♂ Swimming
Dara Torres (4) ♂ Swimming
Evelyn Ashford (4) ♂ Athletics
Janet Evans (4) ♂ Swimming
Lisa Leslie (4) ♂ Basketball
Pat McCormick (4) ♂ Diving
Sanya Richards-Ross (4) ♂ Athletics
Serena Williams (4) ♂ Tennis
**Simone Biles** (4) ♂ Gymnastics
Biles's phenomenal medal tally in Olympics and World Championships is greater than any other US gymnast.

Tamika Catchings (4) ♂ Basketball
Teresa Edwards (4) ♂ Basketball
Venus Williams (4) ♂ Tennis

# Around the World When You Turned 35

It's a big news day every day, somewhere in the world. Here are the stories that the media thought you'd want to read in the year of your 35th birthday.

✦ Black September murder Israeli athletes at Olympics
✦ Thalomide victims win compensation in court
✦ WWII Japanese soldier ends hideout
✦ Ceylon becomes Sri Lanka
✦ Uganda expels Asians
✦ Cannibalism is used to survive airplane crash in Andes
✦ Olympics in Munich
✦ Japan hosts Winter Olympics
✦ Miners go on strike in England
✦ Cameroon becomes independent
✦ Earthquake kills 1,000 in Turkey
✦ Three gunmen open fire in Tel Aviv airport
✦ Burundi genocide leaves 500,000 dead
✦ Iraq hit by earthquake that kills 5,000
✦ Mount Fuji avalanche kills 19
✦ Demark joins the European Community
✦ Brazilian driver becomes youngest Formula One winner
✦ Smallpox epidemic occurs in Yugoslavia
✦ Thousands die in Nicaraguan earthquake
✦ Biological weapons are banned
✦ IRA intensifies violence with several bombings
✦ Martial law is declared in the Philippines
✦ Military coup succeeds in Ghana
✦ Fire in Osaka nightclub kills 115
✦ UK begins training the Special Air Services

# Drinks of the Sixties

For many of those slipping from adolescence into adulthood, your choice of drink says a lot about you. Sophisticated or down-to-earth? A classic, or something to make a statement? In the years that follow, the drinks might change, but the decision remains the same! Here's what was behind a sixties bar.

Falstaff beer
**Rusty Nail cocktail**
Rumored to be a favorite drink of the Rat Pack.

Hull's Cream Ale
Stinger cocktail
Rheingold Extra Dry Lager
Gunther's Beer
Lone Star Beer
The Gimlet cocktail
The Grasshopper cocktail
**Little King's Cream Ale**
Best known for its miniature seven-ounce bottles.

Mai Thai cocktail
Genesee Cream Ale
**Storz Beer**
From Nebraska, Storz was "Brewed for the beer pro."

**Iron City Beer**
Iron City is reputed to have introduced the first twist-off bottle cap in 1963.

Golden Dream cocktail
**Mint Julep cocktail**
It's the official drink of the Kentucky Derby, with around 120,000 served over the weekend.

Koch's Light Lager Beer
Arrow 77 Beer
Daiquiri cocktail
Manhattan cocktail
Sterling Premium Pilsner
Carling Black Label
Hamm's Beer
Old fashioned cocktail

# Seventies Game Shows

With enough water under the bridge since the 1950s scandals, producers of seventies game shows injected big money into new formats and revamped favorites, some of them screened five nights a week. How many did you cheer on from the couch?

High Rollers 🏆 (1974-88)

Gambit 🏆 (1972-81)

**The New Treasure Hunt** 🏆 (1973-82)
Perhaps the best-known episode of this show saw a woman faint when she won a Rolls Royce–that she later had to sell in order to pay the taxes.

The Cross-Wits 🏆 (1975-87)

Hollywood Squares 🏆 1966-2004)

**The Newlywed Game** 🏆 (1966-2013)
Show creator Chuck Barris also made "3's a Crowd"– the show in which men, their secretaries and their wives competed. The public wasn't happy.

**Pyramid** 🏆 (1973-present)
Thanks to inflation and rival prizes, the $10,000 Pyramid in 1973 didn't last long: from 1976 it was raised in increments to its current peak of $100,000.

Dealer's Choice 🏆 (1974-75)

Sports Challenge 🏆 (1971-79)

Tattletales 🏆 (1974-84)

It's Your Bet 🏆 (1969-73)

Celebrity Sweepstakes 🏆 (1974-77)

Rhyme and Reason 🏆 (1975-76)

Three On A Match 🏆 (1971-74)

The Match Game 🏆 (1962-present)

Sale of the Century 🏆 (1969-89)

**The Dating Game** 🏆 (1965-99)
The Dating Game–known as Blind Date in many international versions–saw many celebrity appearances before they became well-known, including the Carpenters and Arnold Schwarzenegger.

# Popular Boys' Names

**40**

Just as middle age crept up unnoticed, so the most popular names also evolved. The traditional choices—possibly including yours—are fast losing their appeal to new parents.

Michael
Jason
Christopher
David
James
John
Robert
**Brian**
1977 marks the sixth year Brian held 8th place, his personal best. Sadly for Brian, it was downhill from here.

Matthew
Joseph
Daniel
William
Kevin
Joshua
Jeremy
Ryan
Eric
Timothy
Jeffrey
Richard
Anthony
Thomas
Steven
Andrew
Mark
Charles
Scott

**Rising and falling stars:**
Sliding out of the Top 100 for ever: Johnny, Rodney and Jimmy. Bursting through the door: Wesley, in the highest position he'll reach (66th).

# Popular Girls' Names

It's a similar story for girls' names. Increasing numbers are taking their infant inspiration from popular culture. The worlds of music, film and theater are all fertile hunting grounds for indecisive new parents.

Jennifer
**Melissa**
Melissa took runner-up spot in 1977, and held it for three years. But she couldn't quite depose Jennifer.

Amy
Jessica
Heather
Angela
Michelle
Kimberly
Amanda
Kelly
Sarah
Lisa
Elizabeth
Stephanie
Nicole
Christina
Rebecca
Jamie
Shannon
Laura
Mary
Julie
Erin
Andrea
Crystal
Rachel

**Rising and falling stars:**
Girls we welcomed for the first time this year: Sabrina, Kristy and Vanessa. Names we'd never see in the Top 100 again: Brenda, Tamara, Sharon and Beth.

# NBA Champions Since You Were Born

These are the winners of the NBA Finals in your lifetime—and the number of times they've taken the title.

- Philadelphia Warriors (2)
- Baltimore Bullets (1)
- Minneapolis Lakers (5)
- Rochester Royals (1)
- Syracuse Nationals (1)
- **Boston Celtics (17)**
  1966: After the Lakers won Game 1 of the NBA Finals, the Celtics named their star Bill Russell player-coach. He was the first black coach in the NBA. The Celtics responded by winning the series.

- St. Louis Hawks (1)
- Philadelphia 76ers (2)
- New York Knicks (2)
- Milwaukee Bucks (2)
- **Los Angeles Lakers (12)**
  1980: With Kareem Abdul-Jabbar out with an injury, Lakers' 20-year-old rookie Magic Johnson started at center in the clinching Game 6 and scored 42 points and snared 15 rebounds.

- **Golden State Warriors (4)**
  2015: LeBron James and Stephen Curry, the stars of the teams that faced off in the 2015 NBA Finals, were both born in the same hospital in Akron, Ohio.

- Portland Trail Blazers (1)
- Washington Bullets (1)
- Seattle SuperSonics (1)
- Detroit Pistons (3)
- Chicago Bulls (6)
- Houston Rockets (2)
- San Antonio Spurs (5)
- Miami Heat (3)
- Dallas Mavericks (1)
- Cleveland Cavaliers (1)
- Toronto Raptors (1)

# Fashion in the Seventies

The decade that taste forgot? Or a kickback against the sixties and an explosion of individuality? Skirts got shorter (and longer). Block colors and peasant chic vied with sequins and disco glamor. How many of your seventies outfits would you still wear today?

### Wrap dresses
Diane von Fürstenberg said she invented the silent, no-zipper wrap dress for one-night stands. "Haven't you ever tried to creep out of the room unnoticed the following morning? I've done that many times."

Tube tops
### Midi skirt
In 1970, fashion designers began to lower the hemlines on the mini skirt. This change wasn't welcomed by many consumers. Women picketed in New York City with "stop the midi" signs.

Track suit, running shoes, soccer jerseys
Cowl neck sweaters
His & hers matching outfits
Cork-soled platform shoes
Caftans, Kaftans, Kimonos and mummus
Prairie dresses
Cuban heels
Gaucho pants
Chokers and dog collars as necklaces
Birkenstocks
Tennis headbands
Turtleneck shirts
Puffer vests
Long knit vests layered over tops and pants
Military surplus rucksack bags
### "Daisy Dukes" denim shorts
Daisy's revealing cut-off denim shorts in The Dukes of Hazzard caught the attention of network censors. The answer for actor Catherine Bach? Wear flesh-colored pantyhose–just in case.

Yves Saint Laurent
Shrink tops
Bill Gibb

# Drinks of the Seventies

Breweries were bigger, and there were fewer of them. Beers were lighter. But what could you (or your parents) serve with your seventies fondue? How about a cocktail that's as heavy on the double-entendre as it was on the sloe gin? Or perhaps match the decade's disco theme with a splash of blue curaçao?

**Amber Moon cocktail**
Features an unbroken, raw egg and featured in the film
Murder on the Orient Express.

Billy Beer
Rainier Beer
Point Special Lager
Tequila Sunrise cocktail
Regal Select Light Beer
Stroh's rum
Long Island Iced Tea cocktail
Merry Widow cocktail
Shell's City Pilsner Premium Beer
Brass Monkey cocktail
The Godfather cocktail
Brown Derby
Sea-Breeze cocktail

**Schlitz**
This Milwaukee brewery was the country's largest in the late sixties and early seventies. But production problems were followed by a disastrous ad campaign, and by 1981 the original brewery was closed.

Alabama Slammer cocktail
Golden Cadillac cocktail
Harvey Wallbanger cocktail
Red White & Blue Special Lager Beer
Lite Beer from Miller

**Coors Banquet Beer**
A beer that made the most of its initial limited distribution network by floating the idea of contraband Coors. The idea was so successful that Coors smuggling became central to the plot of the movie Smokey and the Bandit.

# US Open Tennis

Across the Open Era and the US National Championship that preceded it, these men won between the year you turned 19 (matching the youngest ever champ, Pete Sampras) and 38 (William Larned's age with his seventh win, in 1911).

| | |
|---|---|
| 1956 | Ken Rosewall |
| 1957 | Malcolm Anderson |
| 1958 | Ashley Cooper |
| 1959-60 | Neale Fraser |
| 1961 | Roy Emerson |
| 1962 | Rod Laver |
| 1963 | Rafael Osuna |
| 1964 | Roy Emerson |
| 1965 | Manuel Santana |
| 1966 | Fred Stolle |
| 1967 | **John Newcombe** |

Newcombe was George W. Bush's drinking companion the day in 1976 when Bush was charged with driving under the influence of alcohol.

| | |
|---|---|
| 1968 | Arthur Ashe |
| 1969 | Rod Laver |
| 1970 | Ken Rosewall |
| 1971 | Stan Smith |
| 1972 | Illie Nastase |
| 1973 | John Newcombe |
| 1974 | Jimmy Connors |
| 1975 | **Manuel Orantes** |

Orantes came back from 5-0 down in the 4th set of the semifinal to win the 4th and 5th sets and upset top-seeded Jimmy Connors in the final.

# Books of the Decade

Family, friends, TV, and more: there are as many midlife distractions as there are books on the shelf. Did you get drawn in by these bestsellers, all published in your thirties?

| | |
|---|---|
| 1967 | Rosemary's Baby by Ira Levin |
| 1967 | The Arrangement by Elia Kazan |
| 1967 | The Confessions of Nat Turner by William Styron |
| 1968 | Airport by Arthur Hailey |
| 1968 | Couples by John Updike |
| 1969 | The Godfather by Mario Puzo |
| 1969 | Slaughterhouse-Five by Kurt Vonnegut |
| 1969 | Portnoy's Complaint by Philip Roth |
| 1969 | The French Lieutenant's Woman by John Fowles |
| 1970 | Love Story by Erich Segal |
| 1970 | One Hundred Years of Solitude by Gabriel Garcia Marquez |
| 1971 | The Happy Hooker: My Own Story by Xaviera Hollander |
| 1971 | The Exorcist by William Peter Blatty |
| 1972 | Watership Down by Richard Adams |
| 1972 | The Joy of Sex by Alex Comfort |
| 1972 | Fear and Loathing in Las Vegas by Hunter S. Thompson |
| 1973 | Fear of Flying by Erica Jong |
| 1973 | Gravity's Rainbow by Thomas Pynchon |
| 1974 | Jaws by Peter Benchley |
| 1974 | The Front Runner by Patricia Nell Warren |
| 1975 | The Eagle Has Landed by Jack Higgins |
| 1975 | Shōgun by James Clavell |
| 1975 | Ragtime by E.L. Doctorow |
| 1976 | Roots by Alex Haley |
| 1976 | The Hite Report by Shere Hite |

# Around the World When You Turned 40

International stories from farflung places—but did they appear on your radar as you clocked up four decades on the planet?

✦ Australia's worst rail accident kills 83 in Sydney
✦ Anwar Sadat visits Israel
✦ Panama gains control of Panama Canal
✦ Indira Gandhi resigns as prime minister
✦ Post-Franco Spain holds elections
✦ Tenerife planes collide: 583 die in world's worst air disaster
✦ Chaplin dies
✦ Brazil's Pele retires from soccer
✦ Public trade unions strike in UK
✦ Race riots erupt in Bermuda
✦ Bucharest is shaken by earthquake
✦ Quebec adopts French as official language
✦ Israel elects Begin as prime minister
✦ Cyclone in India results in thousands dead and millions homeless
✦ Elizabeth II celebrates Jubilee (25 years of rule)
✦ Terrorists set off three bombs in Moscow
✦ Volcano erupts in Zaire
✦ Last execution by guillotine in France
✦ Blizzard causes houses to collapse in Northern Japan
✦ War begins between Vietnam and Cambodia
✦ Dutch school taken over by terrorists
✦ Virginia Wade wins Wimbledon
✦ Libya and Egypt go to war
✦ Japan's Mount Usu erupts
✦ Last natural smallpox case discovered

# Across the Nation

Here are the headline stories from across the country in the year you hit 40.

- VHS machines arrive on the market
- Apple II released
- President Jimmy Carter inaugurated (right)
- Atari 2600 gaming system released
- Son of Sam killer arrested
- NASA launches Voyager I and Voyager II
- New York City blackout
- Elvis Presley died
- Authority over Panama Canal returned to Panama
- Trans Alaska Pipeline starts pumping oil
- Beverly Hills Supper Club catches fire
- President Carter pardons Vietnam draft dodgers
- President Carter warns about curtailing oil consumption
- Seattle Slew wins the Triple Crown
- Dam in Georgia fails, killing 39 people
- First GPS signal received and decoded
- Space Shuttle makes first test flight
- Commodore PET begins sales
- Radio Shack offers TRS-80 to consumers
- Comedian Steve Martin asks to be excused
- I love New York ad begins
- Two baseball players first give each other a "high five"
- Snow falls in Miami for the first and last known time
- A.J. Foyt takes 1st place in the Indy 500 for the 4th time
- Disco craze takes America

*Born this year:*
- Rapper Kanye West
- Boxer Floyd Mayweather Jr.
- Author John Green
- Actress Liv Tyler

"Jimmy Who is Running for What!?" a newspaper in Jimmy Carter's home state of Georgia asked after he announced his intention to run for president. But an effective national strategy, his status as an "outsider" and favorable media coverage took the former peanut farmer and nuclear physicist all the way to the White House.

# The Biggest Hits When You Were 40

Big tunes for a big birthday: how many of them enticed your middle-aged party guests onto the dance floor?

Leo Sayer ♪ When I Need You
Fleetwood Mac ♪ Dreams
Thelma Houston ♪ Don't Leave Me This Way
The Marshall Tucker Band ♪ Heard It in a Love Song
David Soul ♪ Don't Give Up on Us
The Eagles ♪ Hotel California
Glen Campbell ♪ Southern Nights
The Bee Gees ♪ Stayin' Alive
The Emotions ♪ Best of My Love
Queen ♪ We Are the Champions
Rose Royce ♪ Car Wash
Crystal Gayle ♪ Don't It Make
My Brown Eyes Blue
Eric Clapton ♪ Lay Down Sally
Linda Ronstadt ♪ Blue Bayou
Stevie Wonder ♪ Sir Duke
Bonnie Tyler ♪ It's a Heartache
The Floaters ♪ Float On
Kenny Rogers ♪ Lucille
Bill Conti ♪ Gonna Fly Now
(Theme from Rocky)
Marvin Gaye ♪ Got to Give It Up (Part 1)
Supertramp ♪ Give a Little Bit
The Commodores ♪ Brick House
Dolly Parton ♪ Here You Come Again
Al Stewart ♪ Year of the Cat

# Popular Food in the 1970s

From fads to ads, here's a new collection of dinner party dishes and family favorites. This time it's the seventies that's serving up the delights—and some of us are still enjoying them today!

Watergate Salad
Black Forest cake
Chex Mix
Cheese Tid-Bits
Dolly Madison Koo-koos (cupcakes)
**Life Cereal**
"I'm not gonna try it. You try it. Let's get Mikey...he hates everything." Three on- and off-screen brothers, one memorable ad that ran for much of the seventies.

**The Manwich**
"A sandwich is a sandwich, but a manwich is a meal," the ads announced in 1969.

Tomato aspic
Bacardi rum cake
Impossible pies
Zucchini bread
Oscar Mayer bologna
Poke Cake made with Jell-O
Libbyland Dinners
**Reggie! Bar**
Named after New York Yankees' right fielder Reggie Jackson and launched as a novely, Reggie! Bars were on sale for six years.

Hostess Chocodiles
Polynesian chicken salad
Salmon mousse
Cheese log appetizer
Gray Poupon Dijon Mustard
**Tootsie Pop**
So how many licks does it take to get to the center of a Tootsie Pop? 364, and that's official: it was tested on a "licking machine."

# Cars of the 1970s

A decade of strikes, federal regulations, foreign imports, oil crises, safety and quality concerns: car sales were up overall, but the US industry was under pressure like never before. Iconic new models to debut include the Pontiac Firebird and the outrageous, gold-plated Stutz Blackhawk.

| 1940 | **Chrysler New Yorker**<br>When is a New Yorker not a New Yorker? The eighth generation of this upscale car bore little resemblance to the 1940 launch models. Yet in 1970, the New Yorker was barely middle-aged: they lived on until 1997. |
|------|------|
| 1948 | Ford F-Series |
| 1959 | General Motors Cadillac Coupe de Ville |
| 1959 | Chrysler Plymouth Valiant |
| 1960 | Chrysler Dodge Dart |
| 1961 | **General Motors Oldsmobile Cutlass**<br>The Cutlass outsold any other model in US for four consecutive years, notching up nearly 2 million sales. |
| 1962 | General Motors Chevrolet Nova |
| 1965 | General Motors Chevrolet Caprice |
| 1965 | Ford LTD |
| 1967 | General Motors Pontiac Firebird |
| 1968 | BMW 2002 |
| 1970 | Chrysler Dodge Challenger |
| 1970 | General Motors Chevrolet Monte Carlo |
| 1970 | General Motors Chevrolet Vega |
| 1970 | American Motors Corporation Hornet |
| 1970 | Ford Maverick |
| 1971 | Nissan Datsun 240Z |
| 1971 | **Stutz Blackhawk**<br>These luxury automobiles started at a cool $22,000 ($150,000 today); the first car sold went to Elvis. Among the many other celebrity Blackhawk owners was Dean Martin; one of his three models sported the vanity plate DRUNKY. He crashed it. |
| 1971 | Ford Pinto |
| 1973 | Honda Civic |
| 1975 | Ford Granada |
| 1978 | Ford Fiesta |

# US Banknotes

The cast of US banknotes hasn't changed in your lifetime, giving you plenty of time to get to know them. (Although if you have a lot of pictures of James Madison and Salmon P. Chase around the house, you might want to think about a visit to the bank.)

**Fifty cent paper coin** (1862-1876) 🖼 Abraham Lincoln
These bills were known as "shinplasters" because the quality of the paper was so poor that they could be used to bandage leg wounds during the Civil War.

**One dollar bill** (1862-1869) 🖼 Salmon P. Chase
The US Secretary of Treasury during Civil War, Salmon P. Chase is credited with putting the phrase "In God we trust" on US currency beginning in 1864.

**One dollar bill** (1869-present) 🖼 George Washington
Some bills have a star at the end of the serial number. This means they are replacement bills for those printed with errors.

One silver dollar certificate (1886-96) 🖼 Martha Washington
**Two dollar bill** (1862-present) 🖼 Thomas Jefferson
Two dollar bills have a reputation of being rare, but there are actually 600 million in circulation in the US.

Five dollar bill (1914-present) 🖼 Abraham Lincoln
Ten dollar bill (1914-1929) 🖼 Andrew Jackson
Ten dollar bill (1929-present) 🖼 Alexander Hamilton
Twenty dollar bill (1865-1869) 🖼 Pocahontas
Twenty dollar bill (1914-1929) 🖼 Grover Cleveland
Twenty dollar bill (1929-present) 🖼 Andrew Jackson
Fifty dollar bill (1914-present) 🖼 Ulysses S. Grant
**One hundred dollar bill** (1914-1929) 🖼 Benjamin Franklin
The one hundred dollar bill has an expected circulation life of 22.9 years while the one dollar bill has an expected circulation life of just 6.6 years.

Five hundred dollar bill (1918-1928) 🖼 John Marshall
Five hundred dollar bill (1945-1969) 🖼 William McKinley
One thousand dollar bill (1918-1928) 🖼 Alexander Hamilton
One thousand dollar bill (1928-1934) 🖼 Grover Cleveland
Five thousand dollar bill (1918-1934) 🖼 James Madison
Ten thousand dollar bill (1928-1934) 🖼 Salmon P. Chase

# Male Olympic Gold Medalists in Your Lifetime

These are the male athletes that have scooped the greatest number of individual and team gold medals at the Summer Olympics in your lifetime.

Michael Phelps (23) ♂ Swimming (right)
Carl Lewis (9) ♂ Athletics
**Mark Spitz** (9) ♂ Swimming
For 36 years, Spitz's 7-gold-medal haul at the 1972 Munich Olympics was unbeaten; Michael Phelps finally broke the spell with his eighth gold in Beijing.

Matt Biondi (8) ♂ Swimming
Caeleb Dressel (7) ♂ Swimming
Ryan Lochte (6) ♂ Swimming
Don Schollander (5) ♂ Swimming
Gary Hall Jr. (5) ♂ Swimming
Aaron Peirsol (5) ♂ Swimming
Nathan Adrian (5) ♂ Swimming
Tom Jager (5) ♂ Swimming
**Al Oerter Jr.** (4) ♂ Athletics
Four out of four: Oerter won Olympic gold medals in the discus in every Games from 1956-1968. He fought injuries that required him to wear a neck brace for the 1964 Tokyo Olympics—but he still set an Olympic record.

Greg Louganis (4) ♂ Diving
Jason Lezak (4) ♂ Swimming
John Naber (4) ♂ Swimming
Jon Olsen (4) ♂ Swimming
Lenny Krayzelburg (4) ♂ Swimming
Matt Grevers (4) ♂ Swimming
**Michael Johnson** (4) ♂ Athletics
Once the fastest man in the world over 200 meters, Johnson took 15 minutes to walk the same distance in 2018 following a mini-stroke—but took it as a sign that he'd make a full recovery.

**Harrison Dillard** (4) ♂ Athletics
Dillard—known as "Bones" for his skinny build—aspired to match the feats of his idol, Jesse Owens. And he did, becoming the only man to win gold as a sprinter and a hurdler.

Between 2000 and 2016, Michael Phelps won 28 Olympic medals, including 23 gold and 16 for individual events. That's 10 more than his nearest competitor, Larisa Latynina, a gymnast of the Soviet Union who took her last gold medal fifty years earlier.

# Winter Olympics Venues Since You Were Born

Unless you're an athlete or winter sports fan, the Winter Olympics can slip past almost unnoticed. These are the venues; can you remember the host countries and years?

Lillehammer
Cortina d'Ampezzo
Oslo
Salt Lake City
Sapporo
**Albertville**
The last Games to be held in the same year as the Summer Olympics, with the next Winter Olympics held two years later.

Turin
Grenoble
Beijing
Sarajevo
Lake Placid
Sochi
**Innsbruck (twice)**
This usually snowy city experienced its mildest winter in 60 years; the army transported snow and ice from the mountains. Nevertheless, twelve years later, the Winter Olympics were back.

Squaw Valley
Nagano
**St Moritz**
The first Winter Olympics to be held for 12 years and named the 'Games of Renewal'; Japan and Germany were not invited.

Calgary
Vancouver
PyeongChang

**Answers:** Lillehammer: Norway, 1994; Cortina d'Ampezzo: Italy, 1956; Oslo: Norway, 1952; Salt Lake City: USA, 2002; Sapporo: Japan, 1972; Albertville: France, 1992; Turin: Italy, 2006; Grenoble: France, 1968; Beijing: China, 2022; Sarajevo: Yugoslavia, 1984; Lake Placid: USA, 1980; Sochi: Russia, 2014; Innsbruck: Austria, 1964; Squaw Valley: USA, 1960; Nagano: Japan, 1998; St Moritz: Switzerland, 1948; Calgary: Canada, 1988; Innsbruck: Austria, 1976; Vancouver: Canada, 2010; PyeongChang: South Korea, 2018

# Fashion in the Eighties

Eighties fashion was many things, but subtle wasn't one of them. Influences were everywhere from aerobics to Wall Street, from pop princesses to preppy polo shirts. The result was chaotic, but fun. How many eighties throwbacks still lurk in your closet?

Stirrup pants
Ralph Lauren
Ruffled shirts
Jean Paul Gaultier
**Acid wash jeans**
Stone washing had been around a while, but the acid wash trend came about by chance—Rifle jeans of Italy accidentally tumbled jeans, bleach, and pumice stone with a little water. The result? A fashion craze was born.

Camp collar shirt with horizontal stripes
Thierry Mugler
Oversized denim jackets
Scrunchies
**"Members Only" jackets**
Members Only military-inspired jackets were marketed with the tagline "When you put it on...something happens."

Paper bag waist pants
Pleated stonewash baggy jeans
Cut-off sweatshirts/hoodies
Vivienne Westwood
Azzedine Alaia
Shoulder pads
Dookie chains
Leg warmers
Bally shoes
Jordache jeans
Calvin Klein
Windbreaker jackets
**Ray-Ban Wayfarer sunglasses**
Popularized by Tom Cruise in the movie Risky Business.
Parachute pants
Jumpsuits

# World Buildings

Some of the most striking and significant buildings in the world sprang up when you were between 25 and 50 years old. How many do you know?

| | |
|---|---|
| 1962 | CIBC Tower, Montreal |
| 1963 | Esso Tower, La Défense |
| 1964 | **Yoyogi National Gymnasium, Tokyo**<br>The Yoyogi National Gymnasium was designed and built for the 1964 Olympics. It is famous for its suspension roof design. |
| 1965 | Shalom Meir Tower, Tel-Aviv |
| 1966 | CN Tower (Edmonton) |
| 1967 | Habitat 67 |
| 1968 | Museum of Art of São Paulo Assis Chateaubriand |
| 1969 | Gateway House, Manchester |
| 1970 | Cathedral of Brasília |
| 1971 | Näsinneula tower, Tampere, Finland |
| 1972 | Olympiastadion, Munich |
| 1973 | **The Sydney Opera House**<br>The iconic Sydney Opera House sits on the tip of Bennelong Point—on a site that previously homed a tram shed. |
| 1974 | Shinjuku Mitsui Building, Tokyo |
| 1975 | First Canadian Place, Toronto |
| 1976 | The CN Tower, Toronto |
| 1977 | **The Centre Pompidou, Paris**<br>The Centre Pompidou, known locally as Beaubourg, is considered the "inside-out" landmark—its structure and mechanical services are outside the building. |
| 1978 | Sunshine 60, Tokyo |
| 1979 | Kuwait Towers, Kuwait City |
| 1981 | Sydney Tower |
| 1982 | First Canadian Centre, Calgary |
| 1983 | Teresa Carreño Cultural Complex, Caracus |
| 1984 | Deutsche Bank Twin Towers, Frankfurt |
| 1985 | Exchange Square, Hong Kong |
| 1986 | **Baha'i Lotus Temple, New Delhi**<br>The Lotus Temple is open to all faiths to come worship, but no images, pictures, sermons, or even musical instruments are permitted. |

# Across the Nation

How many of these big national stories do you remember unfolding live on TV and radio?

- ✦ Politician commits suicide during live press conference
- ✦ Minnesota Twins win the World Series
- ✦ New York Giants win the Super Bowl
- ✦ "Your brain on drugs" ad airs
- ✦ Reagan says "Mr. Gorbachev, tear down this wall"
- ✦ Prozac is prescribed
- ✦ California condors are preserved from extinction
- ✦ Black Monday strikes the stock market
- ✦ Senator Gary Hart drops out of presidential race over scandal
- ✦ Robert Bork rejected by Senate for Supreme Court seat
- ✦ Televangelist Jim Bakker forced to resign over affair
- ✦ Flight 255 crashes, killing 156, but a 4-year-old girl survives
- ✦ John Paul II visits
- ✦ Whittier Narrows earthquake strikes
- ✦ Child rescued from a water well in Texas
- ✦ DNA used to convict criminal
- ✦ Squirrel closes down NASDAQ
- ✦ No-smoking rule in federal buildings takes effect
- ✦ Basketball's Kareem Abdul-Jabbar scores his 36000th point
- ✦ Radio station starts 24-hour sports format
- ✦ Healthcare worker sentenced for poisoning 24 patients
- ✦ NFL players go on strike
- ✦ Murderous ex-employee causes Flight 1771 crash, kills all on board
- ✦ Video compact discs available

*Born this year:*
- ☞ Actor Zac Efron
- ☞ Rapper Kendrick Lamar
- ☞ American footballer Colin Kaepernick

# Around the World When You Turned 50

Here is the last set of international headlines in the book, and they're not so long ago (comparatively speaking).

+ Fiji becomes a republic
+ West German pilot lands Cessna in Red Square
+ Ferry capsizes off coast of Belgium
+ Supernova that can be seen without telescopes appears
+ Hurricane-force wind strikes English coast
+ Single European Act comes in effect
+ Diesel train sets speed record in UK
+ France announces plans to build Disneyland Paris
+ Terrorists kidnap Terry Waite
+ UK elects Thatcher for third time
+ Series of bomb attacks kill over 100 in Sri Lanka
+ Hungerford shooting rampage occurs in UK
+ Fire in the Underground kills 31 in London
+ Nazi Klaus Barbie found guilty of crimes against humanity
+ Bus passengers murdered by terrorists in India
+ Supertyphoon Nina devastates the Philippines
+ Horrific ferry accident in Manila kills 4,000
+ President of Ecuador is kidnapped, later released
+ Rugby World Cup begins in New Zealand
+ Martial Law ends in Taiwan after almost 40 years
+ F4 tornado strikes Edmonton, Alberta
+ Rudolf Hess dies in prison
+ Elizabeth II opens Order of the Garter to include women
+ Iranian pilgrims clash with authorities at Mecca
+ New Zealand becomes a Nuclear-Free Zone

# Kentucky Derby Winners

These are the equine and human heroes from the "most exciting two minutes of sport" during your thirties and forties. Did any of them make you rich?

| | |
|---|---|
| 1967 | Proud Clarion (Bobby Ussery) |
| 1968 | Forward Pass (Ismael Valenzuela) |
| 1969 | Majestic Prince (Bill Hartack) |
| 1970 | **Dust Commander (Mike Manganello)**<br>Diane Crump became the first female jockey this year. |
| 1971 | Canonero II (Gustavo Ávila) |
| 1972 | Riva Ridge (Ron Turcotte) |
| 1973 | **Secretariat (Ron Turcotte)**<br>Secretariat and Sham, both racing in the 1973 Kentucky Derby, had what still stand as the two fastest times ever in the race. Secretariat broke the track records at all three Triple Crown races. |
| 1974 | Cannonade (Angel Cordero Jr.) |
| 1975 | Foolish Pleasure (Jacinto Vasquez) |
| 1976 | Bold Forbes (Angel Cordero Jr.) |
| 1977 | Seattle Slew (Jean Cruguet) |
| 1978 | **Affirmed (Steve Cauthen)**<br>Affirmed won the Triple Crown, with Alydar finishing second in all three Triple Crown races. |
| 1979 | Spectacular Bid (Ronnie Franklin) |
| 1980 | **Genuine Risk (Jacinto Vasquez)**<br>Genuine Risk became the first female horse to win the Kentucky Derby since 1915. |
| 1981 | Pleasant Colony (Jorge Velasquez) |
| 1982 | Gato Del Sol (Eddie Delahoussaye) |
| 1983 | Sunny's Halo (Eddie Delahoussaye) |
| 1984 | Swale (Laffit Pincay Jr.) |
| 1985 | Spend A Buck (Angel Cordero Jr.) |
| 1986 | **Ferdinand (Bill Shoemaker)**<br>54-year-old Bill Shoemaker became the oldest jockey to ever win the Kentucky Derby. |

# World Series Champions Since You Were Born

These are the winners of the Commissioner's Trophy and the number of times they've been victorious in your lifetime.

- Detroit Tigers (3)
- New York Yankees (21)
- Cincinnati Reds (4)
- St. Louis Cardinals (8)
- Cleveland Indians (1)
- New York Giants (1)
- Brooklyn Dodgers (1)
- Milwaukee Braves (1)
- **Los Angeles Dodgers (6)**
  1988: Dodgers' Kirk Gibson, battling injuries, hit a game-winning home run in his only at-bat of the 1988 World Series.
- Pittsburgh Pirates (3)
- Baltimore Orioles (3)
- **New York Mets (2)**
  1969: The Mets had never finished above 9th in their division.
- Oakland Athletics (4)
- Philadelphia Phillies (2)
- Kansas City Royals (2)
- **Minnesota Twins (2)**
  1991: Both teams had finished in last place the previous season.
- Toronto Blue Jays (2)
- Atlanta Braves (2)
- Florida Marlins (2)
- Arizona Diamondbacks (1)
- Anaheim Angels (1)
- Boston Red Sox (4)
- Chicago White Sox (1)
- San Francisco Giants (3)
- **Chicago Cubs (1)**
  2016: The Cubs' first World Series win since 1908.
- Houston Astros (1)
- Washington Nationals (1)

# Books of the Decade

By our forties, most of us have decided what we like to read. But occasionally a book can break the spell, revealing the delights of other genres. Did any of these newly published books do that for you?

| | |
|---|---|
| 1977 | The Thorn Birds by Colleen McCullough |
| 1977 | The Women's Room by Marilyn French |
| 1978 | Eye of the Needle by Ken Follett |
| 1978 | The World According to Garp by John Irving |
| 1979 | Flowers in the Attic by V.C. Andrews |
| 1979 | The Hitchhiker's Guide to the Galaxy by Douglas Adams |
| 1979 | Sophie's Choice by William Styron |
| 1980 | Rage of Angels by Sidney Sheldon |
| 1980 | The Bourne Identity by Robert Ludlum |
| 1980 | The Covenant by James Michener |
| 1981 | The Hotel New Hampshire by John Irving |
| 1981 | Noble House by James Clavell |
| 1981 | An Indecent Obsession by Colleen McCullough |
| 1982 | The Color Purple by Alice Walker |
| 1982 | Space by James A. Michener |
| 1983 | Pet Sematary by Stephen King |
| 1983 | Hollywood Wives by Jackie Collins |
| 1984 | You Can Heal Your Life by Louise Hay |
| 1984 | Money: A Suicide Note by Martin Amis |
| 1985 | The Handmaid's Tale by Margaret Atwood |
| 1985 | White Noise by Don DeLillo |
| 1985 | Lake Wobegon Days by Garrison Keillor |
| 1986 | It by Stephen King |
| 1986 | Wanderlust by Danielle Steele |

# Vice Presidents in Your Lifetime

The linchpin of a successful presidency, the best springboard to become POTUS, or both? Here are the men—and woman—who have shadowed the most powerful person in the world in your lifetime.

| | |
|---|---|
| 1933-41 | **John Garner** <br> His nickname was Cactus Jack and he lived to be 98 years old, making him the longest-lived VP to date. |
| 1941-45 | Henry A. Wallace |
| 1945 | Harry S. Truman |
| 1949-53 | **Alben W. Barkley** <br> He died of a heart attack during a speech at a political convention three years after the end of his term. |
| 1953-61 | Richard Nixon |
| 1961-63 | Lyndon B. Johnson |
| 1965-69 | Hubert Humphrey |
| 1969-73 | **Spiro Agnew (right)** |
| 1973-74 | Gerald Ford |
| 1974-77 | Nelson Rockefeller |
| 1977-81 | Walter Mondale |
| 1981-89 | **George H. W. Bush** <br> He is only the second vice president to win the presidency while holding the office of vice president. |
| 1989-93 | **Dan Quayle** <br> Quayle famously misspelled potato ("potatoe") |
| 1993-2001 | **Al Gore** <br> This VP won the Nobel Peace Prize in 2007, following in the footsteps of two other former vice presidents. |
| 2001-09 | Dick Cheney |
| 2009-17 | Joe Biden |
| 2017-20 | **Mike Pence** <br> In the 90s, Pence took a break from politics to become a conservative radio talk show and television host. |
| 2020- | Kamala Harris |

Spiro Agnew resigned in 1973, the second VP to quit in America's history (the first was John Calhoun in 1932). He stepped down after being charged with tax evasion and taking bribes. He covered his legal debts with a loan from friend Frank Sinatra. In 1983 he was compelled to repay $268,000: the money he had taken in bribes, plus interest.

# British Prime Ministers in Your Lifetime

These are the occupants of 10 Downing Street, London, during your lifetime (not including Larry the resident cat). The list features two women, three knights, and two who returned for a second go.

| | |
|---|---|
| 1935-37 | Stanley Baldwin |
| 1937-40 | Neville Chamberlain |
| 1940-45 | Winston Churchill |
| 1945-51 | Clement Attlee |
| 1951-55 | **Sir Winston Churchill**<br>Churchill was made an honorary citizen of the United States in 1963, one of only eight to receive this honor. |
| 1955-57 | Sir Anthony Eden |
| 1957-63 | **Harold Macmillan**<br>Macmillan was the scion of a wealthy publishing family. He resigned following a scandal in which a minister was found to have lied about his relationship with a 19-year-old model. Macmillan died aged 92; his last words were, "I think I will go to sleep now." |
| 1963-64 | Sir Alec Douglas-Home |
| 1964-70 | Harold Wilson |
| 1970-74 | Edward Heath |
| 1974-76 | Harold Wilson |
| 1976-79 | James Callaghan |
| 1979-90 | **Margaret Thatcher**<br>In 1994, Thatcher was working late in a Brighton hotel, preparing a conference speech. A bomb—planted weeks earlier by the IRA five stories above—detonated, devastating the hotel. Five were killed; Thatcher was unscathed. The conference went ahead. |
| 1990-97 | John Major |
| 1997-2007 | Tony Blair |
| 2007-10 | Gordon Brown |
| 2010-16 | David Cameron |
| 2016-19 | Theresa May |
| 2019- | Boris Johnson |

# Things People Do Now (Part 2)

Imagine your ten-year-old self being given this list of today's mundane tasks and habits—and the puzzled look on your face!

+ Listen to a podcast
+ Go "viral" or become social media famous
+ Watch YouTube
+ Track the exact location of family members via your smartphone
+ Watch college football playoffs
+ Have drive-thru fast food delivered to your door
+ Check reviews before trying a new restaurant or product
+ Use LED light bulbs to save on your electric bill
+ Wear leggings as pants for any occasion
+ Use hashtags (#) to express an idea or show support
+ Join a CrossFit gym
+ Use a Forever stamp to send a letter
+ Carry a reusable water bottle
+ Work for a company with an "unlimited" paid time off policy
+ "Binge" a TV show
+ Marry a person of the same sex
+ Take your shoes off when going through airport security
+ Take a selfie
+ Use tooth-whitening strips
+ Feed babies and kids from food pouches
+ Buy recreational marijuana from a dispensary (in some states)
+ Store documents "in the cloud" and work on them from any device
+ Clean up after your pets using compostable waste bags
+ Buy free-range eggs and meat at the grocery store

# A Lifetime of Technology

It's easy to lose sight of the breadth and volume of life-enhancing technology that became commonplace during the 20th Century. Here are some of the most notable advances to be made in the years you've been an adult.

| | |
|---|---|
| 1957 | Laser |
| 1958 | Microchip |
| 1960 | Global navigation satellite system |
| 1962 | Red LED |
| 1963 | **Computer mouse** <br> The inventor of the computer mouse patented it in 1963. However, by the time the mouse became commercially available in the 1980s, his patent had expired. |
| 1969 | Laser printer |
| 1971 | Email |
| 1972 | Video games console (Magnavox Odyssey) |
| 1973 | Mobile phone |
| 1974 | Universal Product Code |
| 1979 | Compact disc |
| 1982 | **Emoticons** <br> The inventor of the smiley emoticon hands out "Smiley" cookies every September 19th—the anniversary of the first time it was used. |
| 1983 | Internet |
| 1986 | Mir Space Station |
| 1988 | **Internet virus** <br> The first Internet worm was specifically designed to crack passwords. Its inventor was the son of the man who invented computer passwords. |
| 1989 | World Wide Web |
| 1992 | Digital hand-sized mobile phone |
| 1998 | Google |
| 1999 | Wi-Fi |
| 2000 | Camera phone |
| 2001 | Wikipedia |
| 2004 | Facebook |
| 2007 | Apple iPhone |
| 2009 | Bitcoin |

# The Biggest Hits
# When You Were 50

Fifty: an age when your musical taste is largely settled and modern music can lose its appeal…but how many do you know and how many do you like?

Cutting Crew 🎵 (I Just) Died in Your Arms
Bon Jovi 🎵 Livin' on a Prayer
U2 🎵 I Still Haven't Found
What I'm Looking For
Billy Idol 🎵 Mony Mony
Randy Travis 🎵 Forever and Ever, Amen
Whitesnake 🎵 Here I Go Again
Janet Jackson 🎵 Control
INXS 🎵 Need You Tonight
Bobby Brown 🎵 Girlfriend
Reba McEntire 🎵 The Last One to Know
Lisa Lisa and Cult Jam 🎵 Head to Toe
Prince 🎵 Sign O' the Times
T'Pau 🎵 Heart and Soul
Crystal Gayle 🎵 Straight to the Heart
Janet Jackson 🎵 Let's Wait Awhile
Depeche Mode 🎵 Strange Love
Luther Vandross 🎵 Stop to Love
John Cougar Mellencamp 🎵 Cherry Bomb
George Michael 🎵 I Want Your Sex
Jody Watley 🎵 Looking for a New Love
Crowded House 🎵 Don't Dream It's Over
Aerosmith 🎵 Dude (Looks Like a Lady)
Fleetwood Mac 🎵 Little Lies
Los Lobos 🎵 La Bamba

# Grand Constructions

Governments around the world spent much of the 20th century nation building (and rebuilding), with huge civil engineering projects employing new construction techniques. Here are some of the biggest built between the ages of 25 and 50.

| | |
|---|---|
| 1962 | Dulles Internationl Airport, US |
| 1963 | O'Hare International Airport, US |
| 1964 | Volga-Baltic Waterway, Russia |
| 1965 | Kuma-Manych Canal, Russia |
| 1966 | **Almondsbury Interchange, UK**<br>This interchange is unremarkable by US standards, built on four levels to maximize traffic flow. Thanks to its big footprint, there are only three in the UK; Dallas alone has seven. |
| 1967 | Lion Rock Tunnel, Hong Kong |
| 1968 | Nanjing Yangtze River Bridge, China |
| 1970 | Flathead Tunnel, US |
| 1971 | Azadi Tower, Iran |
| 1972 | Snowy Mountains Scheme, Australia |
| 1973 | Chesapeake Bay Bridge, US |
| 1974 | Charles de Gaulle Airport, France |
| 1975 | Orange-Fish River Tunnel, South Africa |
| 1976 | **Sonnenberg Tunnel, Switzerland**<br>A 5,000-ft road tunnel built to double up as a 20,000-capacity nuclear shelter. Blast doors weigh 350 tons... but take 24 hours to close. |
| 1977 | Guoliang Tunnel, China |
| 1978 | West Gate Bridge, Australia |
| 1979 | Genting Sempah Tunnel, Malaysia |
| 1980 | Reichsbrücke, Austria |
| 1981 | Tjörn Bridge, Scandanavia |
| 1982 | Abu Dhabi International Airport, Abu Dhabi |
| 1983 | Queen Alia International Airport, Jordan |
| 1984 | Tennessee-Tombigbee Waterway, US |
| 1985 | Penang Bridge, Malaysia |
| 1986 | National Waterway 1, India |

# Popular Food in the 1980s

The showy eighties brought us food to dazzle and delight. Food to make us feel good, food to share and food to go. Some innovations fell by the wayside, but many more can still be found in our baskets forty years later.

### Hot Pockets
Hot Pockets were the brainchild of two brothers, originally from Iran. Their invention was launched as the Tastywich before being tweaked to become the Hot Pockets enjoyed by millions.

Bagel Bites
Crystal Light
Steak-Umms
Sizzlean Bacon
Potato skins appetizers
Tofutti ice cream

### Hi-C Ecto Cooler
Hi-C has been around for a very long time, but the Ecto Cooler dates back to the Ghostbusters movie hype of the 1980s.

Hot buttered O's
Knorr Spinach Dip
Original New York Seltzer
Blondies

### Blackened Redfish
The trend for blackening redfish prompted fish stocks to drop so low that commercial fishing for the species was banned in Louisiana.

Bartles & Jaymes Wine Coolers
Fruit Wrinkles
Stuffed mushrooms appetizers

### TCBY Frozen Yogurt
TCBY originally stood for "This Can't Be Yogurt."

Sushi
Fajitas
Capri Sun
Jell-O Pudding Pops

### Lean Cuisine frozen meals
Lean Cuisine is an FDA-regulated term, so all Lean Cuisine frozen meals need to be within the limit for saturated fat and cholesterol.

# Eighties Symbols of Success

In the flamboyant era of Dallas and Dynasty there were many ways to show that you, too, had really made it. Forty years on, it's fascinating to see how some of these throwbacks are outdated or available to nearly everyone, while others are still reserved for today's wealthy peacocks.

BMW car
Cellular car phone
Rolex watch
**Cosmetic surgery**
In 1981 there were 1,000 liposuction procedures performed. That number increased to 250,000 by 1989.

VCR
"Home theater" projection TV
In-ground pool
AKC-registered dog
McMansion
Pagers/"beeper"
Aprica stroller
Home intercom system
Heart-shaped Jacuzzi tub
**NordicTrack**
This machine was originally called the Nordic Jock but was renamed due to compaints from women's rights groups.

Cruise vacation
**Restaurant-standard kitchen appliances**
A popular commercial stove produced enough heat to warm an average three-bedroom home. It was the energy equivalent of six residential stoves.

Ronald Reagan-style crystal jelly bean jar on your desk
Apple or Commodore 64 home computer
Volvo Station Wagon
Gordon Gekko-style "power suit"
Owning a horse or riding lessons for your children
Private jet
Tennis bracelet
Monogrammed clothes and accessories

Launched in 1980, the Apple III personal computer seen here went on sale for a hefty $4,000 and up, the equivalent of over $13,000 today. It didn't sell well and was soon withdrawn (unlike the Apple II, which went on to sell more than 5 million units).

# The Transportation Coils

This novel issue of more than 50 definitive stamps first appeared on post in the early eighties, and became a favorite of collectors for its mono color engraved images of transportation methods past and present. Stamps carrying the printing plate number are particularly treasured. Here's a selection you may remember.

1 c 🔳 Omnibus
2 c 🔳 Locomotive
3 c 🔳 Handcar
4 c 🔳 **Stagecoach**

Coaches have been ferrying people and mail between US towns and cities since the late 18th century.

5 c 🔳 Motorcycle
5.5c 🔳 **Star Route Truck**

Star routes were 19th century mail routes on which carriers bid to make deliveries.

6 c 🔳 Tricycle
7.4 c 🔳 Baby Buggy
10 c 🔳 Canal Boat
11 c 🔳 Caboose
12.5 c 🔳 Pushcart
13 c 🔳 Patrol Wagon
15 c 🔳 Tugboat
17 c 🔳 Electric Auto
17 c 🔳 Dog Sled
17.5 c 🔳 Racing car
18 c 🔳 Surrey
20 c 🔳 Cog Railway
21 c 🔳 Railway Mail Car
23 c 🔳 Lunch Wagon
24.1 c 🔳 Tandem Bike
25 c 🔳 Bread Wagon
32 c 🔳 Ferry Boat
$1 🔳 **Sea Plane**

The US Navy bought its first sea plane in 1911: a Curtiss Model E, with a range of 150 miles.

# Eighties Game Shows

By the eighties, game shows had their work cut out to compete against the popularity of new drama and talk shows. Still, an injection of celebrity glamour and dollar bills—alongside hours to be filled on new cable TV channels—ensured their survival. Here are the biggies.

Double Dare 🏆 (1986-2019)
Remote Control 🏆 (1987-90)
Scrabble 🏆 (1984-93)
**The Price Is Right** 🏆 (1972-present)
"Come on down!"—perhaps the best-known game show catchphrase of all time. One 2008 contestant was even happier than usual to do just that after 3 chips dropped into the Plinko all hit the $10,000 jackpot. Fluke? No, wires used to rig the result when filming ads hadn't been removed. She was allowed to keep the $30,000.

Family Feud 🏆 (1976-present)
**Press Your Luck** 🏆 (1983-86)
A show perhaps best remembered for the contestant Michael Larson, who memorized the game board and engineered a winning streak worth over $110,000. It wasn't cheating—Larson kept the winnings—but the game was swiftly reformulated.

Chain Reaction 🏆 1980-present)
Blockbusters 🏆 (1980-87)
Win, Lose, or Draw 🏆 (1987-90)
On The Spot 🏆 (1984-88)
Jeopardy! 🏆 (1964-present)
Card Sharks 🏆 (1978-present)
**Wheel of Fortune** 🏆 (1975-present)
Hostess Vanna White is estimated to clap 600 times a show; that's around 4,000,000 times since she began in 1982.

Fandango 🏆 (1983-88)
Body Language 🏆 (1984-86)
Jackpot! 🏆 (1974-90)

# Popular Boys' Names

Not many of these boys' names were popular when you were born. But how many more of them are now in your twenty-first century family?

**Michael**
Michael might not know it yet, but his 44-year reign as the most popular name is nearly over: by 1999, Jacob will have wrestled control.

Jacob
Matthew
Christopher
Joshua
Nicholas
Andrew
Brandon
Austin
Tyler
Daniel
Joseph
Zachary
David
John
Ryan
James
Anthony
William
Justin
Jonathan
Alexander
Robert
Kyle
Christian
Jordan

**Rising and falling stars:**
Cole, Angel, Mason and Alejandro are in; Taylor, Dustin, Bradley, Mitchell and Edward are out.

# Popular Girls' Names

It's a similar story for girls' names: only Elizabeth featured in the 30 most popular names for your year of birth. How long will it be before we turn full circle and Mary, Shirley, and Barbara make a comeback?

Emily
Jessica
Ashley
Sarah
Hannah
Samantha
Taylor
Alexis
Elizabeth
Madison
Megan
Kayla
Rachel
Lauren
Alyssa
Amanda
Brianna
Jennifer
Victoria
Brittany
Nicole

**Morgan**
Morgan entered the Top 100 in 1987; climbed to this peak of 22nd, and slid out again by 2013.

Stephanie
Jasmine
Rebecca
Abigail

**Rising and falling stars:**
Say hello to Autumn, Sophia and—for one year only—Michaela. Wave goodbye to Monica, Kristen, Shannon and Crystal.

# Game Show Hosts of the Seventies and Eighties

Here is the new generation of hosts: bow-tied, wide-smiled men to steer family favorites through tumultuous times. Astonishingly, one or two are still holding the cards.

John Charles Daly ✖ What's My Line (1950-1967)
Garry Moore ✖ To Tell The Truth (1969-1976)
Chuck Woolery ✖ Love Connection (1983-1994)
Bob Barker ✖ The Price Is Right (1972-2007)
**Pat Sajak** ✖ Wheel of Fortune (1981-)
Sajak took the crown for the longest-reigning game-show host of all time in 1983, when his 35-year reign surpassed that of Bob Barker as host of The Price is Right.

Peter Tomarken ✖ Press Your Luck (1983-86)
Gene Rayburn ✖ The Match Game (1962-1981)
**Alex Trebek** ✖ Jeopardy! (1984-2020)
At the time of his death in 2020, Trebek had hosted more than 8,200 episodes of the show.

Dick Clark ✖ Pyramid (1973-1988)
Richard Dawson ✖ Family Feud (1976-1995)
Peter Marshall ✖ Hollywood Squares (1966-1981)
Howard Cosell ✖ Battle of the Network Stars (1976-1988)
Marc Summers ✖ Double Dare (1986-1993)
Tom Kennedy ✖ Name That Tune (1974-1981)
Bert Convy ✖ Tattletales (1974-78; 1982-84)
Ken Ober ✖ Remote Control (1987-1990)
Jim Lange ✖ The Dating Game (1965-1980)
Wink Martindale ✖ Tic-Tac-Dough (1978-1985)
**Art Fleming** ✖ Jeopardy! (1964-1975; 1978-79)
Host for the original version, Fleming declined to host the comeback in 1983. His friend Pat Sajak took the job.

Jack Narz ✖ Concentration (1973-78)
Dennis James ✖ The Price Is Right (1972-77)
Jim Perry ✖ $ale of the Century (1983-89)
John Davidson ✖ Hollywood Squares (1986-89)
Ray Combs ✖ Family Feud (1988-1994)
Mike Adamle ✖ American Gladiators (1989-1996)

# TV News Anchors of the Seventies and Eighties

The explosion in cable channels that began with CNN in 1980 brought a host of fresh presenters to join the ranks of trusted personalities that bring us the news. How many of them do you remember?

**Dan Rather** ♟ (CBS)
"Kenneth, what's the frequency?" Those were the words of the man who attacked Rather in 1986. It took a decade before the message was decoded; his assailant wanted to block the beams he believed TV networks were using to target him.

Peter Jennings ♟ (ABC)
Tom Brokaw ♟ (NBC)
Ted Koppel ♟ (ABC)
Bill Beutel ♟ (ABC)
Jessica Savitch ♟ (NBC)
Connie Chung ♟ (NBC)
Diane Sawyer ♟ (CBS/ABC)
Sam Donaldson ♟ (ABC)
**Barbara Walters** ♟ (ABC)
Walters was a popular pioneer; the first woman to co-host and anchor news programs, reaching 74 million viewers with her interview of Monica Lewinsky.

Frank Reynolds ♟ (ABC)
Jane Pauley ♟ (NBC)
Roger Grimsby ♟ (ABC)
Roger Mudd ♟ (CBS/NBC)
Garrick Utley ♟ (NBC)
Bernard Shaw ♟ (CNN)
Frank McGee ♟ (NBC)
Ed Bradley ♟ (CBS)
Larry King ♟ (CNN)
Kathleen Sullivan ♟ (ABC/CBS/NBC)
Jim Lehrer ♟ (PBS)
**Robert MacNeil** ♟ (PBS)
In 1963, MacNeil had a brief exchange of words with a man leaving the Texas School Book Depository; to this day, it is uncertain whether this was Lee Harvey Oswald.

# FIFA World Cup: Down to the Last Four in Your Life

Here are the teams that have made the last four of the world's most watched sporting event in your lifetime (last year in brackets). The US men's team has reached the semifinals once, back in 1930.

France ⚽ (2018, winner)
**Croatia** ⚽ (2018, runner-up)
During a 2006 match against Australia, Croatian player Josip Šimunić was booked three times due to a referee blunder.

Belgium ⚽ (2018, 3rd)
**England** ⚽ (2018, 4th)
In the run-up to the 1966 World Cup, hosted and won by England, the trophy was held to ransom. An undercover detective with fake banknotes arrested the crook; a dog named Pickles found the trophy under a bush.

Brazil ⚽ (2014, 4th)
Germany ⚽ (2014, winner)
Argentina ⚽ (2014, runner-up)
Netherlands ⚽ (2014, 3rd)
Spain ⚽ (2010, winner)
Uruguay ⚽ (2010, 4th)
Italy ⚽ (2006, winner)
Portugal ⚽ (2006, 4th)
Turkey ⚽ (2002, 3rd)
Korean Republic ⚽ (2002, 4th)
Sweden ⚽ (1994, 3rd)
Bulgaria ⚽ (1994, 4th)
Poland ⚽ (1982, 3rd)
Russia ⚽ (1966, 4th)
Czech Republic (as Czechoslovakia) ⚽ (1962, runner-up)
**Chile** ⚽ (1962, 3rd)
The 1962 World Cup saw the 'Battle of Santiago' between Chile and Italy. The first foul occurred 12 seconds into the game, a player was punched in the nose, and police intervened several times.

Serbia (as Yugoslavia) ⚽ (1962, 4th)
Hungary ⚽ (1954, runner-up)
Austria ⚽ (1954, third)

# Books of the Decade

Our final decade of books are the bookstore favorites from your fifties. How many did you read...and can you remember the plot, or the cover?

| | |
|---|---|
| 1987 | Patriot Games by Tom Clancy |
| 1987 | Beloved by Toni Morrison |
| 1987 | The Bonfire of the Vanities by Tom Wolfe |
| 1988 | The Cardinal of the Kremlin by Tom Clancy |
| 1988 | The Sands of Time by Sidney Sheldon |
| 1989 | Clear and Present Danger by Stephen R. Covey |
| 1989 | The Pillars of the Earth by Ken Follett |
| 1990 | The Plains of Passage by Jean M. Auel |
| 1990 | Possession by A.S. Byatt |
| 1990 | Four Past Midnight by Stephen King |
| 1991 | The Firm by John Grisham |
| 1991 | The Kitchen God's Wife by Amy Tan |
| 1991 | Scarlett by Alexandra Ripley |
| 1992 | The Bridges of Madison County by Robert James Waller |
| 1992 | The Secret History by Donna Tartt |
| 1993 | The Celestine Prophecy by James Redfield |
| 1993 | Like Water for Chocolate by Laura Esquivel |
| 1994 | The Chamber by John Grisham |
| 1994 | Disclosure by Michael Crichton |
| 1995 | The Horse Whisperer by Nicholas Evans |
| 1995 | The Lost World by Michael Crichton |
| 1995 | The Rainmaker by John Grisham |
| 1996 | Angela's Ashes by Frank McCourt |
| 1996 | Bridget Jones's Diary by Helen Fielding |
| 1996 | Infinite Jest by David Foster Wallace |

April 17, 1970: Jim Lovell is brought aboard a helicopter—the last of the three astronauts from the Apollo 13 mission to be lifted from the floating Command Module.

# Apollo Astronauts

Whatever your personal memories of the events, the moon landings are now woven into our national story—but not all of the Apollo astronauts who made the journey are equally well known. Twelve landed; twelve remained in lunar orbit. Gus Grissom, Ed White, and Roger B Chaffee died in training.

*Landed on the moon:*

Alan Bean

**Alan Shepard**
He was the oldest person to walk on the moon at age 47.

Buzz Aldrin

Charles Duke

David Scott

Edgar Mitchell

Eugene Cernan

Harrison Schmitt

James Irwin

John Young

Neil Armstrong

Pete Conrad

*Remained in low orbit:*

Al Worden

**Bill Anders**
He is the photographer responsible for the iconic image Earthrise.

Dick Gordon

Frank Borman

Fred Haise

Jack Swigert

Jim Lovell

Ken Mattingly

Michael Collins

**Ron Evans**
Made the final spacewalk of the program to retrieve film cassettes.

**Stuart Roosa**
On the Apollo 14 mission he carried seeds from 5 species of trees. They were planted across the US and are known as "Moon Trees."

Tom Stafford

# US Open Tennis

And now it's the women's turn. Here are the tournament's victors when you were between the ages of the current "winning window": 16 years (Tracy Austin in 1979), and a venerable 42 years (Molla Mallory in 1926: she won eight times).

| | |
|---|---|
| 1951–53 | Maureen Connolly |
| 1954–55 | Doris Hart |
| 1956 | Shirley Fry Irvin |
| 1957–58 | **Althea Gibson**<br>Gibson became the first black winner of the US Open. |
| 1959 | Maria Bueno |
| 1960–61 | Darlene Hard |
| 1962 | Margaret Court |
| 1963–64 | Maria Bueno |
| 1965 | Margaret Court |
| 1966 | Maria Bueno |
| 1967 | Billie Jean King |
| 1968 | Virginia Wade |
| 1969–70 | **Margaret Court**<br>Court won both the amateur and open championships in 1969. |
| 1971–72 | Billie Jean King |
| 1973 | **Margaret Court**<br>In 1973, the US Open became the first Grand Slam tournament to offer equal prize money to male and female winners. |
| 1974 | Billie Jean King |
| 1975–78 | **Chris Evert**<br>During the 1975 US Open, Evert beat her long-time rival Martina Navratilova in the semi-final. That evening, Navratilova defected to the United States and subsequently won the US Open four times. |
| 1979 | **Tracy Austin**<br>16-year-old Tracy Austin is the youngest US Open champion ever. |

# The Biggest Hits When You Were 60

We're not reaching back very far for these hits—but unless you're very young at heart, that probably means you won't know very many of them!

Elton John ♪ Candle in the Wind

Puff Daddy and Faith Evans ♪ I'll Be Missing You

Jewel ♪ You Were Meant for Me

Tim McGraw with Faith Hill ♪ It's Your Love

Usher ♪ You Make Me Wanna

Hanson ♪ MMMBop

R. Kelly ♪ I Believe I Can Fly

Will Smith ♪ Men in Black

George Strait ♪ Carrying Your Love with Me

The Verve ♪ Bittersweet Symphony

Meredith Brooks ♪ Bitch

The Wallflowers ♪ One Headlight

Toby Keith ♪ Me Too

Smash Mouth ♪ Walkin' on the Sun

The Backstreet Boys ♪ Quit Playing Games (With My Heart)

Third Eye Blind ♪ Semi-Charmed Life

The Cardigans ♪ Love Fool

Kenny Chesney ♪ She's Got It all

Duncan Sheik ♪ Barely Breathing

Sugar Ray ♪ Fly

Sister Hazel ♪ All For You

Trisha Yearwood and Garth Brooks ♪ In Another's Eyes

Paula Cole ♪ Where Have All the Cowboys Gone

Eric Clapton ♪ Change the World

# Things People Did When You Were Growing Up (Part 2)

Finally, here are more of the things we did and errands we ran as kids that nobody needs, wants, or even understands how to do in the modern age!

✦ Buy cigarettes for your parents at the corner store as a child
✦ Use a pay phone (there was one on almost every corner)
✦ Join a bowling league
✦ Collect cigarette or baseball trading cards
✦ Get frozen meals delivered to your door by the iconic refrigerated yellow Schwan's truck
✦ Attend "Lawn Faiths"/ ice cream socials
✦ Chat with strangers over CB radio
✦ Look up a phone number in the Yellow or White Pages
✦ Visit the Bookmobile for new library books
✦ Have a radio repaired at an appliance/electronics shop
✦ Ride your bike without a helmet
✦ Go to American Bandstand parties
✦ Take part in a panty raid prank
✦ Attend a sock hop
✦ Get milk delivered to your door
✦ Hang out with friends at a pizzeria
✦ Use a rotary phone at home
✦ Use a typewriter
✦ Save your term paper on a floppy disc
✦ Listen to LPs and the newest 45s
✦ Care for a pet rock
✦ Use a card catalogue to find books at the library
✦ Attend a Sadie Hawkins Dance where girls invited the boys
✦ Go disco roller skating

Made in the USA
Monee, IL
28 August 2022

12771675R00067